SERMON IN A SENTENCE

Sermon *in a* Sentence

A Treasury of Quotations
on the Spiritual Life

FROM THE PAPAL
WRITINGS AND ADDRESSES
of
POPE BENEDICT XVI
Priest & Pope

Arranged According to the Virtues of
The Holy Rosary and Other Spiritual Topics

Selected and Arranged by
JOHN P. McCLERNON

Angelico Press

First published in the USA
by Angelico Press 2023

Copyright © 2023 Angelico Press

All excerpts are here used courtesy
of Libreria Editrice Vaticana
© Libreria Editrice Vaticana

For information, address:
Angelico Press, Ltd.

169 Monitor St.
Brooklyn, NY 11222

www.angelicopress.com

ppr 978-1-62138-903-3

cloth 978-1-62138-904-0

Book and cover design
by Michael Schrauzer

"Not only are we restless for God: God is restless for us. God is waiting for us. He is looking for us. He knows no rest, either, until He finds us. God's heart is restless, and that is why He set out on the path towards us—to Bethlehem, to Calvary."   —Pope Benedict XVI

DEDICATION

This work is dedicated to my wonderful and supportive wife, Mary, and to the fruit of our marriage, the five beautiful children Our Lord has blessed us with: Christopher, Clare, Catherine, David and Stephen.

I also wish to thank Pope Benedict XVI—or as he preferred to be called during his retirement years "Father Benedict"—for his long and generous service to the Catholic Church, not just as Pope but also for the many years he served faithfully at the side of his predecessor—St. John Paul II. He will certainly go down as one of the more prominent, if not the greatest, Catholic theologians and thinkers of the 20th and early 21st centuries. He was most definitely a cleric who placed his considerable talents and gifts at the service of Jesus Christ and His Church—as all priests do, with the highest and noblest goal of working toward saving souls and guiding them to their eternal destiny.

As you read, reflect, and pray through this book of quotes from his papal writings and homilies I am confident that Pope Benedict's remarkable intelligence, theological insights, spiritual gifts, and common sense will bless you in your personal relationship with Jesus Christ, and with His Church. He is the real author of this book. It is an honor and privilege to bring his advice and teachings to you in a simple, yet effective way.

John McClernon

CONTENTS

PREFACE

Through his writings Pope Benedict communicates an air of Christian authenticity—one which surely arises from the deep and abiding relationship he has with Our Lord. The clarity and precision of his works serve as a faithful guide for those seeking to strengthen their relationship with God. This volume allows readers to easily access many beautiful excerpts from his writings and homilies as they seek to draw closer to Christ and deepen their life in Him.

During my early college seminary years I first experienced our Holy Father's writings after receiving an edition of *The Spirit of the Liturgy*. A few years later during my theological studies I began to more fully appreciate and enjoy the style with which Pope Benedict instructs. Not only did he accompany me from the printed pages, but being blessed to receive a Roman education, I was often able to hear him teach in person. I often listened to him explain the Sunday Gospel in St. Peter's Square through his weekly Angelus message, and at other times I was spiritually nourished as he preached at Holy Mass. Seeing him in person and listening to him speak helped his other writings come alive. When speaking about my years of university studies, I often say "he was my favorite professor."

One moment in particular stands out to me: it was the day I encountered him most as a professor. In the Paul VI Hall during a general audience the Holy Father was reading from his prepared text, when he proceeded to gently set down his papers, look up at us, and begin teaching his message from the heart—slightly moving his hand up and down for emphasis as he spoke. There was nothing extraordinary about the moment, but it became apparent to all, whether they understood Italian or not, that he was enjoying this opportunity to instruct—and most of all, to help us to better know the Lord.

In this fast-paced world, to create a space for Jesus and to cultivate our friendship with Him will always be a challenge, but now with this collection of simple yet profound insights at our side, our Holy Father can join us on the journey.

Rev. Fr. Corey D. Stanley, S. T. L.
Archdiocese of Oklahoma City

INTRODUCTION

There are many Catholics who greatly desire to deepen their spiritual life and love of Christ by delving into the treasured writings of the Church's great spiritual masters. But how many do so? The culture of today leads us to embrace such busy and distracted lifestyles. All too often the time needed to feed our souls takes a back seat, and we end up spiritually starved and frustrated. The *Sermon in a Sentence* series is designed for just such a person.

Imagine spending personal one-on-one time with Pope Benedict XVI, who is considered by many as the greatest Catholic theologian of the 20th century. Pope Benedict XVI, known as Cardinal Joseph Ratzinger before his election to the papacy, was St. John Paul II's closest confidant and collaborator for that most remarkable papacy, and Benedict would follow the saintly Pope as the Vicar of Christ upon St. John Paul II's death. This collection of short quotes and sayings of Benedict XVI primarily draws upon his papal writings, homilies, and books during his eight-year reign as pope. Praying and reflecting on these spiritual gems one can easily discern the breadth and depth of Benedict's great spiritual knowledge, experience, and ability to communicate a vibrant love of Jesus Christ, of the Catholic Faith, and of our fellow neighbors and those God places in our daily lives. Like John Paul II and many a Pope before him, he was a holy and gifted man chosen by God to lead and shepherd a global flock having to face many cultural obstacles and troubles — notably atheistic, secular, and relativist philosophies that continually infringe upon Christian moral values and traditions in virtually every country on the earth. The Catholic Church of the 20th and early 21st centuries needed

Pope Benedict XVI! This "Sermon" book has been designed to bring the inspiration of his words and writings to you in a very simple yet effective format.

Hundreds of short quotations and sayings taken from the papal writings, addresses, and homilies of Pope Benedict XVI have been classified by the Christian virtues of which they speak and then categorized to complement the Holy Rosary, proceeding from the first joyful mystery (the Annunciation, with its anchor virtue of humility) to the fifth glorious mystery (the Crowning of Mary, with its anchor virtue of love and devotion to Mary). The Luminous Mysteries, introduced by St. John Paul II as an optional addition to the traditional fifteen-decade Rosary, are also included. Additional quotations follow, for use with a Rosary or for separate meditation and spiritual reading. A selection of additional quotations on other spiritual topics follows, bringing the reader a sample of Pope Benedict XVI's insights into such subjects as prayer, the Church, the priesthood, and the Bible.

It is hoped that this little book containing many hundreds of short spiritual "bullets" will serve as an effective introduction to one of our Church's greatest theologians, teachers, and popes. May his teachings and exhortations find a place in your heart and soul, and draw you ever closer to Our Lord Jesus Christ and the Catholic Church He founded, whom Benedict XVI—"Father Benedict"—so generously and effectively served as a priest, bishop, cardinal and pope.

John P. McClernon

ABBREVIATIONS & ACKNOWLEDGMENTS

AE Apostolic Exhortations of the Holy Father Benedict XVI. Obtained from the Vatican website www.vatican.va/holy_father/benedict_xvi/index.htm 2007–2012. Copyright 2007–2012 by Libreria Editrice Vaticana, Vatican City.

C *Church Fathers and Teachers. From Saint Leo the Great to Peter Lombard.* General Audiences March 2008—December 2009. By Pope Benedict XVI. San Francisco, CA: Ignatius Press, 2010. Copyright 2010 by Libreria Editrice Vaticana, Vatican City.

CV *Caritas in Veritate.* Encyclical Letter of the Supreme Pontiff Benedict XVI. To the Bishops, Priests and Deacons, Men and Woman Religious and all the Lay Faithful and all People of Good Will on Integral Human Development in Charity and Truth. June 29, 2009. Obtained from the Vatican website www.vatican.va/holy_father/benedict_xvi/index.htm. Copyright 2009 by Libreria Editrice Vaticana, Vatican City.

D *Deus Caritas Est.* Encyclical Letter of the Supreme Pontiff Benedict XVI. To the Bishops, Priests and Deacons, Men and Women Religious and all the Lay Faithful on Christian Love. December 25, 2005. Obtained from the Vatican website www.vatican.va/holy_father/benedict_xvi/index.htm. Copyright 2005 by Libreria Editrice Vaticana, Vatican City.

G *God's Revolution. World Youth Day and Other Cologne Talks.* By Pope Benedict XVI. San Francisco, CA: Ignatius Press, 2006. Copyright 2006 by Libreria Editrice Vaticana, Vatican City.

H *Holy Men and Women of the Middle Ages and Beyond.*
   General Audiences January 2010–January 2011. By Pope
   Benedict XVI. San Francisco, CA: Ignatius Press, 2012.
   Copyright 2012 by Libreria Editrice Vaticana, Vatican City.

HM Homilies of His Holiness Benedict XVI. April 2012 — Jan-
    uary 2013. Obtained from the Vatican website www.vat-
    ican.va/holy_father/benedict_xvi/index.htm. Copyright
    2012–2013 by Libreria Editrice Vaticana, Vatican City.

I *An Invitation to Faith. An A to Z Primer on the Thought
   of Pope Benedict XVI.* Edited by Jean-Michel Coulet. San
   Francisco, CA: Ignatius Press, 2006. A Giniger Book.
   Published in association with Ignatius Press. Copyright
   2007 Libreria Editrice Vaticana, Vatican City and The
   K.S. Giniger Company.

J *Jesus, the Apostles, and the Early Church.* General Audiences March 2006–February 2007. By Pope Benedict XVI.
   San Francisco, CA: Ignatius Press, 2007. Copyright 2007
   by Libreria Editrice Vaticana, Vatican City.

J1 *Jesus of Nazareth. The Infancy Narratives.* By Joseph
    Ratzinger/Pope Benedict XVI. Translated by Philip J.
    Whitmore. New York City, NY: Image Books, 2012. Copy-
    right 2012 by Libreria Editrice Vaticana, Vatican City.

J2 *Jesus of Nazareth. From the Baptism in the Jordan to the
    Transfiguration.* By Joseph Ratzinger/Pope Benedict XVI.
    New York City, NY: Doubleday Books. 2007. Copyright
    2007 Libreria Editrice Vaticana, Vatican City,

J3 *Jesus of Nazareth. Part Two. Holy Week. From the Entrance
    into Jerusalem to the Resurrection.* By Joseph Ratzinger/
    Pope Benedict XVI. San Francisco, CA: Ignatius Press, 2011.
    Copyright 2011 Libreria Editrice Vaticana, Vatican City.

s   *Spe Salvi*. Encyclical Letter of the Supreme Pontiff Benedict XVI. To the Bishops, Priests and Deacons, Men and Women Religious and all the Lay Faithful on Christian Hope. By Pope Benedict XVI. November 30, 2007. From the Vatican website www.vatican.va/holy_father/benedict_xvi/index.htm. Copyright 2007 Libreria Editrice Vaticana, Vatican City.

POPE BENEDICT XVI
(1927–2022)

The Catholic Church has been blessed over the centuries with many great churchmen to lead and guide it—most notably with the Chair of St. Peter—the Papacy, Vicar of Christ. As the baton has passed from one Pope to another for what is arguably the most challenging, demanding, and daunting responsibility of preserving the apostolic faith and pastoring the worldwide Church of Jesus Christ—numbering as it does today over 1 billion souls—imagine the task of being elected to fill the shoes of St. John Paul II, considered already as one of the greatest Popes, not just in recent Church history, but since the foundation of Christianity. This was the duty entrusted by Our Lord to Cardinal Joseph Ratzinger, who had been one of St. John Paul II's most trusted and closest advisors for decades. Considered by many to be one of the most prominent and knowledgeable theologians of the 20th and early 21st centuries, he would embrace and carry upon his shoulders the same charge placed upon St. Peter and all his successors, a task entrusted to them by none other than Jesus Christ Himself: *"Peter, do you love me? Feed my sheep."*

From a long and respected academic career as a theologian, to serving the Church in many prominent roles within the German Catholic hierarchy, later within the Roman Curia, and eventually to the shepherding of the entire Catholic Church as Pope, Joseph Ratzinger—better known throughout the world as Pope Benedict XVI—always followed the will of God with remarkable faith, hope and charity. Looking back on the 20th- and early 21st-century Church historians will undoubtedly praise and admire the talents, leadership, and spiritual insights seen throughout the 26-year papacy of St. John Paul II. The Catholic Church and entire world was certainly blessed by St. John Paul II, but it should not be forgotten that Cardinal Ratzinger was not just at the side of this saintly pope, but worked directly with him during most of his long and fruitful pontificate. Upon the death of John Paul II Cardinal Ratzinger was elected to the throne of St. Peter, and he would ably place his own unique and gifted talents at the service of souls and the Catholic Church throughout the world.

Joseph Ratzinger was born in Marktl am Inn, within the German diocese of Passau, on April 16, 1927 — which fell on Holy Saturday that year. The Ratzinger family came from a long line of farmers in lower Bavaria, although his father was a career policeman. Joseph's mother was a daughter from a Rimsting artisan family, and had been a cook at a number of hotels before her marriage to his father. The Ratzinger family was to move frequently, but most of his childhood was in Traunstein, a small German village near the Austrian border. This period of pre-WWII Germany had already become troubling, difficult, and harsh on many German Catholics, as the Nazi Party pursued a hostile attitude towards the Church. As a young boy, for example, Joseph was to witness his parish priest being beaten by Nazis soldiers before Mass. Joseph's father was also an outspoken critic of the Nazi regime, which eventually caused the family to move in 1932 to Auschau am Inn, which is located at the foot of Alps. He would later write "How important the action of Christian spouses is. When they are supported by the faith and by a strong spirituality, their courageous commitment for the Church and in the Church becomes natural."

His father would retire seven years later, and the Ratzinger family moved once again back to Traunstein. It was here that Joseph Ratzinger, now a young teenager, would begin studying classical languages, the arts, and sciences. His love for the Catholic faith, fostered by a witness of hope and goodness within the devout Ratzinger family, would also blossom at this time in his life. He would later refer to these years as "Mozartian," complemented and embellished by a strong and vibrant Christian culture and formation within his family and village. The man who would one day be pope was being drawn to serve God and the Church as a priest. Following his 14th birthday in 1941 he was conscripted into the Hitler Youth—as membership was required by law at this age. Joseph had no desire or motivation to be part of this youth group, and refused to attend meetings. During this same year one of Joseph's cousins, a 14-year-old with Down Syndrome, was taken away by the Nazis and murdered as part of a state-sponsored eugenics program.

In 1939 Joseph entered a minor seminary in Traunstein, and remained there until 1943, when he was drafted into the German anti-aircraft corps. His military training also included that of an infantryman. As the Allied front drew closer to his post in 1945, his unit ceased to function and Joseph went back to his family home in Traunstein. At this time the Allied troops were establishing a local headquarters in the Ratzinger household, and due to his still being a German soldier, they placed him in a prisoner of war camp. Joseph would be released a few months later at the end of WWII in May 1945.

At the end of the war Joseph, along with his brother Georg, re-entered the seminary. From 1946 through 1951 he studied philosophy and theology at the University of Freising, and later at the University of Munich. He and Georg were ordained to the priesthood in 1951. He would later write: "In the call to the priestly ministry we meet Jesus and are drawn to Him, struck by His words, His actions, and His person. It is to have the grace to distinguish His voice from so many other voices and to respond like Peter: 'Lord, to whom shall we go? You have the words of eternal life'" (Jn 6:68–69). As a priest he would go on to earn a doctorate in Theology in July 1953, choosing as his thesis "The People and House of God in St. Augustine's Doctrine of Church." After qualifying for university teaching he would also pen a treatise on unique aspects and reflections from the writings of St. Bonaventure, a 13th-century Franciscan Doctor of the Church.

By the end of the 1950s Joseph Ratzinger was establishing himself as one of the leading Catholic theologians of his time, and he continued on this path in what would become a long career as a professor of theology at several German universities, such as the University of Bonn (1959–1963), the University of Münster (1963-1966), and the University of Tübingen (1966–1969). Father Ratzinger was also present as a chief theological advisor to Cardinal Frings, the Archbishop of Cologne, at all four sessions of the Second Vatican Council, which took place during the years 1962 through 1965. The German hierarchy had taken notice of Father Ratzinger's great talents and abilities, and they would place him in various prominent and influential positions within Bishops' Conferences at this time. The final university stop would be at the University of Regensburg, where he held the chair of dogmatics and history of dogma. By this time Father Ratzinger could speak fluently in German, French, Italian, and English—along with a great proficiency in Latin.

In the early 1970s Father Ratzinger would initiate, along with a few other well-known theologians at that time, *Communio*, a highly-respected journal of theology. This quarterly review was in response to the misinformation and confusion in the post-Vatican II Catholic Church. He would also serve as dean and vice-president of the International Theological Commission of the Holy See from 1969 to 1980. On March 25, 1977 Pope Paul VI appointed him Archbishop of Munich & Freising, the first diocesan priest in over 80 years to assume a Bavarian Archdiocese. Bishop Ratzinger took as his motto "Cooperators of the Truth," stating "I chose that motto because in today's world the theme of truth is omitted almost entirely, as something too great for man, and yet everything collapses if truth is missing." Pope Paul VI later that same year made him a Cardinal.

Cardinal Ratzinger would be part of the conclaves in 1978 which elected Pope John Paul I (September) and Pope John Paul II (October). In November 1981 Pope John Paul II would appoint him Prefect for the Congregation for the Doctrine of the Faith, along with primary responsibilities for other Vatican projects such as The Pontifical Biblical Commission and The International Theological Commission. He also was President of the Preparatory Commission for the Catechism of the Catholic Church, which took six years to complete (1986 to 1992). This updated Catechism is considered by many as one of the crowning jewels of the John Paul II papacy.

Due to these and other responsibilities and service to the Church, in February 1982 Cardinal Ratzinger resigned pastoring and governing the Archdiocese of Munich and Freising, and settled in Rome — where he would become one of the most important and influential prelates in the Roman Curia. Cardinal Ratzinger would be one of Pope John Paul II's closest confidants, providing support and guidance to this most remarkable pope's ideas, priorities, major decisions and writings. In 1998 Pope John Paul II approved Cardinal Ratzinger's election as Vice-Dean of the College of Cardinals, and a few years later would name him Dean, or head, of the College of Cardinals. He always had a passion for theological writing, which never waned even in spite of all these Church duties and responsibilities. Among his many publications were *Introduction to Christianity* (1968), *Dogma and Preaching* (1973), *The Ratzinger Report* (1985) and, at the age of 70, he added *Salt of the Earth* (1996). The Congregation for the Doctrine of the Faith, which he headed, also published *Dominus Jesus* for the Jubilee Year 2000 — which re-emphasized the fundamental spiritual truth and Christian teaching that the salvation of human souls can only take place in and through Jesus Christ, and that "salvation is to be found in no one else, for there is no name under heaven given to men by which we must be saved."

Following the death of Pope John Paul II, on April 8, 2005, Cardinal Ratzinger presided over his funeral Mass at the Vatican. On April 19, 2005 his fellow Cardinals elected him to succeed John Paul II as the 265th Bishop of Rome. He later admitted that at a certain point, when he realized that he was a serious candidate, he prayed to God "Please do not do this to me . . . evidently, this time He did not listen to me." This day also marked the feast day of St. Leo IX, who was an important German Pope in medieval times. He chose the name Benedict (Latin for blessed), and explained this decision a few days later in a General Audience: "I remember Pope Benedict XV, that courageous prophet of peace, who guided the Church through turbulent times of war. In his footsteps I place my ministry in the service of reconciliation and harmony between peoples. Additionally, I recall Saint Benedict of Nursia, co-patron of Europe, whose life evokes the Christian roots of Europe. I ask him to help us all to hold firm to the centrality of Christ in our Christian life: May Christ always take first place in our thoughts and actions!"

One of Benedict XVI first actions was to begin the beatification process for John Paul II, which under normal Church procedures could not begin for at least five years after a person's death. Citing exceptional circumstances, on May 13, 2005 — the Feast Day of Our Lady of Fatima and 24th anniversary of the attempt on John Paul II's life — Benedict waived this waiting period in order to initiate the process which would eventually lead to his predecessor's beatification and subsequent canonization.

A consistent theme throughout Benedict's homilies and papal writings was to remind the faithful how everything in the spiritual life depends on friendship with Jesus Christ. "We are all called to open ourselves to this intimate friendship with God," he often stated, "speaking to Him as to a friend, the only One who can make the world both good and happy." The main purpose for three books on the life and teachings of *Jesus of Nazareth* was to help foster and develop the reader's growth in living a vibrant relationship with Our Lord. His first encyclical *God Is Love* (2005) took up this theme, and in his explanation and summary of the encyclical he stated: "If friendship with God becomes for us something ever more important and decisive, then we will begin to love those whom God loves and who are in need of us. God wants us to be friends of his friends and we can be so, if we are interiorly close to them." This personal friendship with God is fueled and maintained by an active prayer life, most especially nourishing the soul with the Bread of Life: "Walk in Christ's light daily through fidelity to personal and liturgical prayer," he wrote, "nourished by meditation on the inspired word of God. Make the daily celebration of the Eucharist the center of your life."

As Pope he also consistently stressed the dangers and spiritual pitfalls of secularization and relativism so prevalent in the world of today. Benedict XVI commonly labelled this a "dictatorship of relativism," claiming that philosophies like these are the greatest challenge facing the Church and humanity, denying as they do any objective or moral truths. In similar fashion to John Paul II, Benedict re-emphasized traditional conservative Catholic teachings and stances on controversial moral issues of our day such as contraception, abortion, and same-sex marriage. In a conference address a few months after his election he stated: "The various forms of the dissolution of marriage today, like free unions, trial marriages and going up to pseudo-matrimonies by people of the same sex, are rather expressions of an anarchic freedom that wrongly passes for true freedom of man ... from here it becomes all the more clear how contrary it is to human love, to the profound vocation of man and woman, to systematically close their union to the gift of life, and even worse to suppress or tamper with the life that is born."

Benedict would follow his first encyclical with two more: *Saved by Hope* (2007) and *Love in Truth* (2009). As Pope he also embarked on numerous apostolic journeys across the world — including Germany (2 visits), Poland, Spain and Turkey all within his first three years. By the end of 2009 he would also visit Brazil, Austria, the United States, Australia, France, and various countries in Africa and the Middle East. Modern materialism — the love of power, possessions and money — he considered as a spiritual and moral plague, comparing it to paganism: "Wake up from selfishness and petty affairs," he often reminded his listeners, "and find time for God and spiritual matters." As pope he would also revive certain Church traditions such as elevating the Tridentine Mass to a more prominent position, and re-establishing the connection of the Catholic faith to the arts and sacred music. True beauty, in the eyes of Benedict, was a path to God.

By 2008 Benedict had reached the age of 83. He had realized from the start that his pontificate would not be very long.

"I too hope in this short reign," he had said, "to be a man of peace." Benedict had been, for sure, a man of peace much after the model of the Prince of Peace, Our Lord. But the physical, emotional and spiritual toll of leading and guiding the Catholic Church had taken a toll on him. Even before his election to the papacy, as Cardinal Ratzinger, he had hoped to retire, submitting a resignation on three separate occasions to Pope John Paul II—who would never accept them. In obedience to John Paul II he continued to serve the Church. Even fourteen years before his election he had suffered a stroke, which temporarily impaired his eyesight at the time. Due to weakness of heart, when a Cardinal, he was also fitted a pacemaker. Citing failing strength to meet the demands of the papacy, the Vatican confirmed in February 2013 that Benedict XVI would resign the papacy before the month was over—the first pope to do so since Gregory XII in 1415. In a statement addressing the Cardinals he gave a brief announcement of the resignation, and declared that he would continue to serve the Church *"through a life dedicated to prayer."*

Benedict XVI would be followed by Pope Francis, an Archbishop from Argentina. The retiring Pope remarked: *"I think South America's day had come. The new Pope, though, is South American and Italian, so he represents both the intertwining of the new and old worlds and the inner unity of history."* As "Pope Emeritus," Benedict XVI would leave the Vatican and temporarily reside at Castel Gandolfo, the papal summer residence, until refurbishment was completed on his retirement home—a monastery in the Vatican Gardens near St. Peter's, where he continued to reside until his passing away on the last day of 2022. His preference was to be referred to as "Father Benedict" after retiring from the papacy. The ailing pope's last words before he died were appropriately: "Lord, I love you!"

"The heart of a happy life, of a true life, is friendship with the Lord Jesus. And this friendship is learned in love for Sacred Scripture, in love for the liturgy, in profound faith, in love for Mary, so as to be ever more truly acquainted with God himself and hence with true happiness, which is the goal of our life." —Pope Benedict XVI

ROSARY
VIRTUES

THE JOYFUL
MYSTERIES

THE FIRST JOYFUL MYSTERY
The Annunciation of Our Lord

HUMILITY

*Whoever humbles himself like this child, he is the
greatest in the kingdom of heaven.* —Matthew 18:4

Let us be brave enough to say: "I do not understand you,
Lord; listen to me, help me to understand." In such a way,
with this frankness which is the true way of praying, of
speaking to Jesus, we express our meager capacity to understand and at the same time place ourselves in the trusting
attitude of someone who expects light and strength from
the One able to provide them. (J 93)

Before the Cross of Christ, the extreme expression of his
self-giving, there is no one who can boast of himself, of
his own self-made justice, made for himself! Elsewhere, re-
echoing Jeremiah, Paul explains this thought, writing, *"Let
him who boasts, boast of the Lord"* (1 Cor 1:31). (J 116)

Faith must constantly express humility before God, indeed,
adoration and praise. (J 117)

A man with public responsibility even in small circles must
always be a man who can listen and learn from what he
hears. (C 23)

Man is exposed to the danger of succumbing to the ancient temptation of seeking to redeem himself by himself—a utopia which in different ways, in twentieth-century Europe, as Pope John Paul II pointed out, has caused "a regression without precedent in the tormented history of humanity." (C 24)

The sign of the new Covenant is humility, hiddenness—the sign of the mustard seed. The Son of God comes in lowliness. (J1 21)

The paradoxical element is God's way of acting ... greatness emerges from what seems in earthly terms small and insignificant, while worldly greatness collapses and falls. (J1 104)

No one is strong enough to travel the entire path of salvation unaided. All have sinned, all need the Lord's mercy, the love of the Crucified One (Rom 3:23-24). (J3 152)

Enlightened by the Word, it is in Bethlehem—the "House of Bread"—that we can always encounter the inconceivable greatness of a God who humbled himself even to appearing in a manger, to giving himself as food on the altar. (G 38)

With our own strength alone, we are incapable of climbing to the loftiness of God. God himself must help us, must "pull" us up. Thus prayer is necessary. (H 56)

Human intelligence is limited and cannot know everything. Only if we were able to know all visible and invisible things perfectly would it be genuinely foolish to accept truths out of pure faith. (H 84)

This is the seal of an authentic experience of the Holy Spirit, the source of every charism: the person endowed with supernatural gifts never boasts of them, never flaunts them, and, above all, shows complete obedience to the ecclesial authority. (H 96)

Our lives contain precious riches that we can lose, and I am not speaking of material riches here. (HM 10-28-12)

I invite you to have a faith that can recognize the wisdom of weakness. . . . Precisely in our limitations and weaknesses as human beings we are called to live conformed with Christ in an all-encompassing commitment. (HM 2-2-13)

God did not withdraw into his heaven but lowered himself to man's experience: a great mystery that succeeds in surpassing every possible expectation. God entered time in a most unthinkable way: by making himself a child and going through the stages of human life. (HM 12-1-12)

The state of blindness has great significance in the Gospels. It represents man who needs God's light, the light of faith, if he is to know reality truly and to walk the path of life. It is essential to acknowledge one's blindness, one's need for this light. (HM 10-28-12)

With the humility of knowing that we are merely grains of wheat, let us preserve the firm certainty that the love of God, incarnate in Christ, is stronger than evil, violence and death. (HM 6-23-11)

We too, all of us, need to learn again to accept God and Jesus Christ as he is, and not the way we want him to be. (HM 4-21-11)

All of us need the conversion which enables us to accept Jesus in his reality as God and man. We need the humility of the disciple who follows the will of his Master. (HM 4-21-11)

Of ourselves, we are too weak to lift up our hearts to the heights of God. We cannot do it. The very pride of thinking that we are able to do it on our own drags us down and estranges us from God. God himself must draw us up, and this is what Christ began to do on the cross. (HM 4-17-11)

God's humility is the extreme form of his love, and this humble love draws us upwards. (HM 4-17-11)

We must bend down, spiritually we must as it were go on foot, in order to pass through the portal of faith and encounter the God who is so different from our prejudices and opinions. (HM 12-24-11)

How often have men and woman tried to build the world by themselves, without or in opposition to God! The result is marked by the drama of ideologies which, in the end, have proven to be against man and his profound dignity. (HM 12-15-11)

True royalty does not consist in a show of power, but in the humility of service; not in the oppression of the weak, but in the ability to protect them and to lead them to life in abundance (Jn 10:10). (HM 11-20-11)

I break the bread of the Word and of the Eucharist with you, in the certainty — shared by us all — that without Christ, the Word and Bread of Life, we can do nothing (Jn 15:5). (HM 10-23-11)

Humility is a virtue that does not enjoy great esteem in the world of today, or indeed of any time. But the Lord's disciples know that this virtue is, so to speak, the oil that makes the process of dialogue fruitful, cooperation possible and unity sincere. (HM 9-25-11)

We often confuse freedom with the absence of bonds, in the conviction that we can manage by ourselves, without God who is seen as a restriction of freedom. This is an illusion. (HM 9-11-11)

The human being is incapable of giving life to himself, he understands himself only by starting from God: it is the relationship with him that gives our humanity consistence and makes our life good and just. (HM 9-11-11)

We cannot follow Jesus on our own. Anyone who would be tempted to do so "on his own," or to approach the life of faith with that kind of individualism so prevalent today, will risk never truly encountering Jesus, or will end up following a counterfeit Jesus. (HM 8-21-11)

We deny God as God by placing ourselves above him, by discarding the whole dimension of love, of interior listening; by no longer acknowledging as real anything but what we can experimentally test and grasp. To think like that is to make oneself God. And to do that is to abase not only God, but the world and oneself, too. (J2 37)

Without heaven, earthly power is always ambiguous and fragile. Only when power submits to the measure and the judgment of heaven — of God, in other words — can it become power for good. And only when power stands under God's blessing can it be trusted. (J2 39)

Any renewal of the Church can be set in motion only through those who keep alive in themselves the same resolute humility, the same goodness that is always ready to serve. (J2 77)

God grants the Evil One a limited power. It can be as a penance for us, in order to dampen our pride, so that we may re-experience the paltriness of our faith, hope, and love and avoid forming too high an opinion of ourselves. (J2 163)

It is only in God and in light of God that we rightly know man. Any "self-knowledge" that restricts man to the empirical and the tangible fails to engage with man's true depth.

Man knows himself only when he learns to understand himself in light of God. (J2 282)

Christ took the lowest place in the world—the Cross—and by this radical humility he redeemed us and constantly comes to our aid. Those who are in a position to help others will realize that in doing so they themselves receive help; being able to help others is no merit or achievement of their own. This duty is a grace. (D 20)

In all humility we will do what we can, and in all humility we will entrust the rest to the Lord. It is God who governs the world, not we. We offer him our service only to the extent that we can, and for as long as he grants us the strength. (D 20)

Good structures help, but of themselves they are not enough. Man can never be redeemed simply from outside.... Science can contribute greatly to making the world and mankind more human. Yet it can also destroy mankind and the world unless it is steered by forces that lie outside it. (S 3)

We are unable to shake off our finitude and ... none of us is capable of eliminating the power of evil, of sin which, as we plainly see, is a constant source of suffering. Only God is able to do this: only a God who personally enters history by making himself man and suffering within history. (S 18)

In the end souls will stand naked before the judge. It no longer matters what they once were in history, but only what they are in truth. (S 20)

No man is an island, entire of itself. Our lives are involved with one another, through innumerable interactions they are linked together. No one lives alone. No one sins alone. No one is saved alone. (S 24)

Development requires a transcendent vision of the person, it needs God: without him, development is either denied, or entrusted exclusively to man, who falls into the trap of thinking he can bring about his own salvation, and ends up promoting a dehumanized form of development. (CV 5)

Human knowledge is insufficient and the conclusions of science cannot indicate by themselves the path towards integral human development. There is always a need to push further ahead: this is what is required by charity in truth. (CV 15)

Without God man neither knows which way to go, nor even understands who he is. In the face of the enormous problems surrounding the development of peoples, which almost make us yield to discouragement, we find solace in the sayings of Our Lord Jesus Christ, who teaches us: "Apart from me you can do nothing" (Jn 15:5) and then encourages us: "I am with you always, to the close of the age" (Mt 28:20). (CV 41)

Intelligence and love are not separate compartments: love is rich in intelligence and intelligence is full of love ... knowledge without love is sterile. (CV 15)

THE SECOND JOYFUL MYSTERY
The Visitation of Elizabeth

LOVE OF NEIGHBOR

You shall love your neighbor as yourself. —Mark 12:31

The Spirit stimulates us to weave charitable relations with all people. Therefore, when we love we make room for the Spirit and give him leeway to express himself fully within us. (J 122)

The Christian must practice charity and almsgiving.... Charity is the greatest of the virtues. (C 35)

Divine love alone prompts us to open our hearts to others and makes us sensitive to their needs, bringing us to consider everyone as brothers and sisters and inviting us to respond to hatred with love and to offense with forgiveness. (C 144 & 145)

Anyone who has discovered Christ must lead others to him. A great joy cannot be kept to oneself. It has to be passed on. (G 13)

Christians are called to seek justice always but to possess an inner impulse to love that goes beyond justice itself. (I 42)

It is much better to be useful and at the disposal of others than to be concerned only with the comforts that are offered to us. (G 14)

God created us all "in his image" (Gen 1:27) and thus honored us with a transcendent dignity. Before God, all men and women have the same dignity, whatever their nation, culture or religion.... The life of every human being is sacred. (G 71 & 75)

The dignity of the person and the defense of the rights which that dignity confers must represent the goal of every social endeavor and of every effort to bring it to fruition. (G 75)

In the heart of the Church a missionary fire must always burn. It must be a constant incentive to make the first proclamation of the Gospel and, wherever necessary, a new evangelization. Christ, in fact, is the most precious good that the men and women of every time and every place have the right to know and love! (H 25)

Precisely by looking at the Crucified One we see . . . how great are the dignity and worth of man. At no other point can we understand how much man is worth, precisely because God makes us so important . . . all human dignity appears in the mirror of the Crucified One. (H 34)

The exercise of authority, at every level, must be lived as a service to justice and charity, in the constant search for the common good. (H 131)

Faith and friendship with Christ create a sense of justice, of the equality of all, of the rights of others, and . . . they create love, charity. And from this charity is born hope, too, the certainty that we are loved by Christ and that the love of Christ awaits us, thereby rendering us capable of imitating Christ and of seeing Christ in others. (H 134)

The more we love God and the more constantly we pray, the better we will succeed in truly loving those who surround us, who are close to us, so that we can see in every person the Face of the Lord, whose love knows no bounds and makes no distinctions. (H 175)

When love is true, by its nature it strives for the good of others, for their greatest possible good. It is not limited merely to respecting the commitments of friendship that have been taken on, but goes further, without calculation or measure. This is precisely what the living, true God did. (HM 12-1-12)

All people have a right to know Jesus Christ and his Gospel: and Christians, all Christians—priests, religious and lay faithful—have a corresponding duty to proclaim the Good News. (HM 10-28-12)

Only someone who actually knows God can lead others to God. Only someone who leads people to God leads them along the path of life. (HM 1-6-12)

The profound sense of the Church's social presence derives from the Eucharist, as is testified by the great social saints who were always great Eucharistic souls. Those who recognize Jesus in the sacred Host, recognize him in their suffering brother or sister, in those who hunger and thirst, who are strangers, naked, sick or in prison; and they are attentive to every person. (HM 6-23-11)

Especially in our time, in which globalization makes us more and more dependent on each other, Christianity can and must ensure that this unity is not built without God, that is, without true Love, which would give way to confusion, individualism and the tyranny of each one seeking to oppress the others. (HM 6-23-11)

The Gospel has always aimed at the unity of the human family. (HM 6-23-11)

We thank all those who, by virtue of their faith and love, place themselves alongside the suffering, thereby bearing definitive witness to the goodness of God himself (HM 4-21-11)

Jesus wanted to identify himself with the poor, with the sick.... Every sick person, every poor person deserves our respect and our love because, through them, God shows us the way to heaven. (HM 11-20-11)

Loving your neighbor is as important as loving God. In fact, a visible sign that the Christian can show the world in order to witness to God's love is love for our brothers and sisters. (HM 10-23-11)

In the spirit of Jesus's teaching something more is needed — an open heart that allows itself to be touched by the love of Christ, and thus gives to our neighbor, who needs us, something more than a technical service: it gives love, in which the other person is able to see Christ, the loving God. (HM 9-25-11)

Being nourished by Christ is the way not to be foreign or indifferent to the fate of the brethren, but rather to enter into the same logic of love and of the gift of the sacrifice of the Cross. (HM 9-11-11)

We cannot encounter Christ and not want to make him known to others. So do not keep Christ to yourselves! Share with others the joy of your faith. The world needs the witness of your faith. (HM 8-21-11)

Is there anything more tragic, is there anything more opposed to belief in the existence of a good God and a Redeemer of mankind, than world hunger? (J2 31)

Zeal and energy must be placed at the service of the protection of human life: all measures that can sustain young couples in forming a family, and the family itself, in the procreation and education of children, are as expedient as ever. (I 89 & 90)

When we come to consider the Sermon on the Mount, we will see that precisely this unconditional Yes to the first tablet of the Ten Commandments also includes the Yes to the second tablet—reverence for man, love of neighbor. (J2 45)

Every instance of trespass among men involves some kind of injury to truth and to love and is thus opposed to God, who is truth and love. (J2 157)

You cannot come into God's presence unreconciled with your brother; anticipating him in the gesture of reconciliation, going out to meet him, is the prerequisite for true worship of God. In so doing, we should keep in mind that God himself—knowing that we human beings stood against him, unreconciled—stepped out of his divinity in order to come toward us, to reconcile us. (J2 158)

I have to become like someone in love, someone whose heart is open to being shaken up by another's need. Then I find my neighbor, or—better—then I am found by him. (J2 197)

Aren't we surrounded by people who have been robbed and battered? The victims of drugs, of human trafficking, of sex tourism, inwardly devastated people who sit empty in the midst of material abundance? All this is of concern to us, it calls us to have the eye and the heart of a neighbor, and to have the courage to love our neighbor. (J2 199)

Everyone must first be healed and filled with God's gifts. But then everyone is also called to become a Samaritan—to follow Christ and become like him. When we do that, we live rightly. We love rightly when we become like him, who loved all of us first (1 Jn 4:19). (J2 201)

Anyone who needs me, and whom I can help, is my neighbor. (D 9)

Seeing with the eyes of Christ, I can give to others much more than their outward necessities. I can give them the look of love which they crave. (D 10)

Only my readiness to encounter my neighbor and to show him love makes me sensitive to God as well. Only if I serve my neighbor can my eyes be opened to what God does for me and how much he loves me. (D 10)

It is often possible to establish a fruitful link between evangelization and works of charity. (D 17)

The command of love of neighbor is inscribed by the Creator in man's very nature. It is also a result of the presence of Christianity in the world, since Christianity constantly revives and acts out this imperative, so often profoundly obscured in the course of time. (D 17)

Charitable activity ... is always concerned with the whole man. Often the deepest cause of suffering is the very absence of God. (D 18)

A world without freedom can by no means be a good world. (S 16)

As Christians we should never limit ourselves to asking: how can I save myself? We should also ask: what can I do in order that others may be saved and that for them too the star of hope may rise? Then I will have done my utmost for my own personal salvation as well. (S 24)

The more we strive to secure a common good corresponding to the real needs of our neighbors, the more effectively we love them. Every Christian is called to practice this charity, in a manner corresponding to his vocation.... This is the institutional path—we might also call it the political path—of charity. (CV 3)

Reason, by itself, is capable of grasping the equality between men and of giving stability to their civic coexistence, but it cannot establish fraternity. This originates in a transcendent vocation from God the Father, who loved us first, teaching us through the Son what fraternal charity is. (CV 9)

It is necessary to cultivate a public conscience that considers food and access to water as universal rights of all human beings, without distinction or discrimination. (CV 13)

Respect for life ... cannot in any way be detached from questions concerning the development of peoples. It is an aspect which has acquired increasing prominence in recent times, obliging us to broaden our concept of poverty and underdevelopment to include questions connected with the acceptance of life, especially in cases where it is impeded in a variety of ways. (CV 14)

Openness to life is at the center of true development. When a society moves towards the denial or suppression of life, it ends up no longer finding the necessary motivation and energy for man's true good. (CV 14)

One of the deepest forms of poverty a person can experience is isolation. If we look closely at other kinds of poverty, including material forms, we see that they are born from isolation, from not being loved or from difficulties in being able to love. (CV 29)

Your own faith serves as a support for the faith of others. (HM 8-21-11)

Christian charitable activity must be independent of parties and ideologies. It is not a means of changing the world ideologically, and it is not at the service of worldly stratagems, but it is a way of making present here and now the love which man always needs. (I 15)

THE THIRD JOYFUL MYSTERY
The Birth of Jesus

SPIRIT OF POVERTY

*Blessed are the poor in spirit, for theirs is
the kingdom of heaven.* —Matthew 5:3

Everything in this world will pass away. In eternity only
Love will remain. (I 48)

Life's difficulties not only reveal how transient and short-
lived life is, but are even shown to serve for identifying and
preserving authentic relations among human beings ... nothing is more precious to the human being than a true friendship. (C 14)

(It is) the figure of Christ in which we learn the truth about
ourselves and thus where to rank all other values, because we
discover their authentic meaning. Jesus Christ is the reference
point that gives light to all other values. (C 65)

This [good] contempt for the world is not a contempt for
Creation, for the beauty and goodness of Creation and of the
Creator, but a contempt for the false vision of the world that is
presented to us and suggested to us precisely by covetousness.
It insinuates that "having" is the supreme value of our being,
of our life in the world, and seems important. And thus it fal-
sifies the creation of the world and destroys the world. (C 89)

The rich person must also find the authentic road of truth,
of love, and thus of an upright life. (C 89)

The renunciation of private property, this freedom from
material things, as well as moderation and simplicity apply in

a radical form only to monks, but the spirit of this renounce-
ment is equal for all. (C 108)

We must not depend on material possessions but instead
must learn renunciation, simplicity, austerity, and moderation.
Only in this way can a supportive society develop and the
great problem of poverty in this world be overcome. (C 108)

How many Christians make haste today, where the things
of God are concerned? Surely if anything merits haste . . . it
is the things of God. (J1 79)

Should this passing world be dearer to us than the Lord for
whom we are actually waiting? (J3 288)

We live in a society in which "having" often prevails over
"being." (H 10)

The witness of Francis, who loved poverty as a means to
follow Christ with dedication and total freedom, continues
to be for us, too, an invitation to cultivate interior poverty
in order to grow in our trust of God by adopting also a
sober lifestyle and a detachment from material goods. (H 20)

Any created thing is nothing in comparison to God and is
worth nothing outside him; consequently, to attain to the
perfect love of God, every other love must be conformed
in Christ to the Divine Love. (H 203)

What makes the soul pure and free is the elimination of
every disorderly dependence on things. All things should
be placed in God as the center and goal of life. (H 204)

One must account to God for one's actions and one's way
of life and seek not to accumulate riches on this earth but,
rather, to live simply and charitably in such a way as to lay
up treasure in Heaven. (H 210)

Human beings have planted in their innermost depths a longing for God ... in him alone can they find true joy and the most complete fulfillment. (H 218)

We want ourselves. We want what we can seize hold of, we want happiness that is within our reach, we want our plans and purposes to succeed. We are so "full" of ourselves that there is no room left for God. And that means there is no room for others either, for children, for the poor, for the stranger. (HM 12-24-12)

It is probably not very often that we make haste for the things of God. God does not feature among the things that require haste. The things of God can wait, we think and we say. And yet he is the most important thing, ultimately the one truly important thing. (HM 12-24-12)

To be disciples of Jesus means not letting ourselves be allured by the worldly logic of power, but bringing into the world the light of truth and God's love. (HM 11-25-12)

Without God, man ultimately chooses selfishness over solidarity and love, material things over values, having over being. We must return to God, so that man may return to being man. (HM 10-4-12)

It is precisely God who liberates our liberty, he frees it from being closed in on itself, from the thirst for power, possessions, and domination; he opens it up to the dimension which completely fulfills it: the gift of self, of love, which in turn becomes service and sharing. (HM 10-4-12)

The restless heart ... is the heart that is ultimately satisfied with nothing less than God, and in this way becomes a loving heart. Our heart is restless for God and remains so. (HM 1-6-12)

There is no lack of difficulties and obstacles, due above all to the hedonistic models that obscure minds and risk uprooting all morality. The temptation has crept in to believe that man's true wealth is not faith, but personal and social power, his intellect, his culture and his capacity to manipulate scientific, technological and social reality. (HM 6-19-11)

People have begun to replace faith and Christian values with presumed riches which ultimately prove to be inconsistent and unable to sustain the great promise of the true, the good, the beautiful and the just that for centuries your ancestors have identified with the experience of faith. (HM 6-19-11)

Let us strip away our fixation on what is material, on what can be measured and grasped. Let us allow ourselves to be made simple by the God who reveals himself to the simple of heart. (HM 12-24-11)

God is generous to us, he offers us his friendship, his gifts, his joy, but often we do not welcome his words, we show greater interest in other things and put our own material concerns, our own interests, first. (HM 10-9-11)

I urge you to root your spiritual life ever more deeply in the Gospel, cultivating your inner life, an intense relationship with God, and detaching yourselves with determination from a certain consumerist and worldly mentality, which is a recurrent temptation in the situation in which we live. (HM 10-9-11)

Relying on his love, do not be intimidated by surroundings that would exclude God and in which power, wealth and pleasure are frequently the main criteria ruling people's lives. You may be shunned along with others who propose higher goals or who unmask the false gods before whom many now bow down. (HM 8-21-11)

When God is regarded as a secondary matter that can be set aside temporarily or permanently on account of more important things, it is precisely these supposedly more important things that come to nothing. It is not just the negative outcome of the Marxist experiment that proves this. (J2 33)

The poor, in their humility, are the ones closest to God's heart, whereas the opposite is true of the arrogant pride of the rich, who rely only on themselves. (J2 75)

The saying of Saint Thérèse of Lisieux about one day standing before God with empty hands, and holding them open to him, describes the spirit of these poor ones of God: They come with empty hands; not with hands that grasp and clutch, but with hands that open and give and thus are ready to receive from God's bountiful goodness. (J2 76)

In order to be the community of Jesus's poor, the Church has constant need of the great ascetics. She needs the communities that follow them, living out poverty and simplicity so as to display to us the truth of the Beatitudes. (J2 77)

Those who mourn are promised comfort; those who are persecuted are promised the Kingdom of God—the same promise that is made to the poor in spirit. The two promises are closely related. The Kingdom of God—standing under the protection of God's power, secure in his love—that is true comfort. (J2 88)

Our faith ... enables us to see God, which binds us with Christ. This is why we pray that, in our concern for goods, we may not lose the Good itself; that even faced with the loss of goods, we may not also lose the Good, which is God. (J2 166)

In the end, man needs just one thing, in which everything else is included; but he must first delve beyond his superficial wishes and longings in order to learn to recognize what it is that he truly needs and truly wants. He needs God. (J2 353 & 354)

It is not the elemental spirits of the universe, the laws of matter, which ultimately govern the world and mankind, but a personal God governs the stars, that is, the universe; it is not the laws of matter and of evolution that have the final say, but reason, will, love—a Person. (s 3)

Faith gives life a new basis, a new foundation on which we can stand, one which relativizes the habitual foundation, the reliability of material income. A new freedom is created with regard to this habitual foundation of life. (s 5)

Love of God leads to participation in the justice and generosity of God towards others. Loving God requires an inner freedom from all possessions and all material goods: the love of God is revealed in responsibility for others. (s 14)

In the parable of the rich man and Lazarus (Lk 16:19-31), Jesus admonishes us through the image of a soul destroyed by arrogance and opulence, who has created an impassible chasm between himself and the poor man; the chasm of being trapped within material pleasures; the chasm of forgetting the other, of incapacity to love. (s 22)

Without the perspective of eternal life, human progress in this world is denied breathing-space. Enclosed within history, it runs the risk of being reduced to the mere accumulation of wealth; humanity thus loses the courage to be at the service of higher goods, at the service of the great and disinterested initiatives called forth by universal charity. (cv 5)

Profit is useful if it serves as a means towards an end that provides a sense both of how to produce it and how to make good use of it. Once profit becomes the exclusive goal, if it is produced by improper means and without the common good as its ultimate end, it risks destroying wealth and creating poverty. (CV 10)

The conviction that man is self-sufficient and can successfully eliminate the evil present in history by his own action has led him to confuse happiness and salvation with imminent forms of material prosperity and social action. (CV 17)

"Our heart is restless until it rests in you," said Saint Augustine at the beginning of his *Confessions*. Yes, man is restless, because whatever is finite is too little. (HM 4-21-11)

THE FOURTH JOYFUL MYSTERY
The Presentation in the Temple

OBEDIENCE

If you love me, you will keep my commandments. —John 14:15

This is the drama of Gethsemane: not my will but yours. It is by transferring the human will to the divine will that the real person is born; it is in this way that we are redeemed. (C 62)

After the original sin, man has tended to do what he likes . . . If each person is self-centered, the social structure cannot function. Only by learning to fit into the common freedom, to share and to submit to it, learning legality, that is, submission and obedience to the rules of the common good and life in common, can society, as well as the *self*, be healed of the pride of being the center of the world. (C 108)

God tells only the truth . . . true authority is reasonable, because God is creative reason. (C 119)

The human being's vocation was to become like God, who created him in his image and likeness. The image of God present in man impels him toward likeness, that is, toward an ever fuller identity between his own will and the divine will. (C 195 & 196)

The "just" are those who inwardly live the ordinances of the law aright—those who walk their path in righteousness, according to the revealed will of God, and open up space for new action by the Lord. (J1 19)

Psalm 1 presents the classic image of the "just" man. We might well think of it as a portrait of the spiritual figure of

Saint Joseph. A just man, it tells us, is one who maintains living contact with the word of God, who "delights in the law of the Lord" (v. 2). (J1 39)

Doing what is right here and now is incumbent on us in the sight of God....To be vigilant is to know that one is under God's watchful eye and to act accordingly. (J3 48)

Standing against the whole flood of filth and evil is the obedience of the Son, in whom God himself suffered, and hence this obedience always infinitely surpasses the growing mass of evil (Rom 5:16-20). (J3 133)

"Filial will" abandons itself totally to the Father's will ... it is Jesus's acceptance of the horror of the Cross, his ignominious experience of being stripped of all dignity and suffering a shameful death, that becomes the glorification of God's name. (J3 156 & 157)

The human will, as created by God, is ordered to the divine will. In becoming attuned to the divine will, it experiences its fulfillment, not its annihilation. (J3 160)

From the Cross, new life comes to us. On the Cross, Jesus becomes the source of life for himself and for all. On the Cross, death is conquered ... his obedience becomes life for all. (J3 166)

God is rightly venerated when we live in obedience to his word and are hence thoroughly shaped by his will. (J3 234)

Keeping one's gaze freely fixed upon God in order to receive from him the criterion of right action and the capacity for it—that is what matters. Vigilance means first of all openness to the good, to the truth, to God. (J3 288)

The secret of holiness is friendship with Christ and faithful obedience to his will. Saint Ambrose said: "Christ is everything for us"; and Saint Benedict warned against putting anything before the love of Christ. (G 48)

Submission becomes union, because he to whom we submit is Love. In this way submission acquires a meaning, because it does not impose anything on us from the outside, but liberates us deep within. (G 59)

The Commandments are the means that the Lord gives us to protect our freedom, both from the internal conditioning of passions and from the external abuse of those with evil intentions. The "noes" of the Commandments are as many "yeses" to the growth of true freedom. (I 16)

The Ten Commandments are not a burden, but a signpost showing the path leading to a successful life. This is particularly the case for the young people....Young people are the future of humanity and the hope of the nations. (G 72 & 74)

It is only in communion with the Church built on the Apostolic succession that obedience to the word of God can be renewed. (H 17)

Always be conformed to God's will, in order to desire and to do everything only and always for his glory. (H 63)

Loving (God) means always doing his will. (H 183)

The law is wisdom. Wisdom is the art of being human, the art of being able to live well and of being able to die well. And one can live and die well only when the truth has been received and shows us the way. (HM 9-1-12)

No one can say: I have the truth — this is the objection raised — and, rightly so, no one can have the truth. It is the truth that possesses us, it is a living thing! We do not possess it but are held by it. Only if we allow ourselves to be guided and moved by the truth, do we remain in it. Only if we are, with it and in it, pilgrims of truth, then it is in us and for us. (HM 9-2-12)

You must not limit yourselves to hearing the Word, you must put it into practice. (HM 9-2-12)

God calls: it is necessary to listen, to receive and to respond to him, like Mary: "Behold, I am the handmaid of the Lord; let it be to me according to your word" (Lk 1:38). (HM 7-15-12)

Friendship is not just about knowing someone, it is above all a communion of the will. It means that my will grows into ever greater conformity with (God's) will. (HM 6-29-11)

Christ's yoke is identical with his friendship. It is a yoke of friendship and therefore "a sweet yoke," but as such it is also a demanding yoke, one that forms us. It is the yoke of his will, which is a will of truth and love. (HM 6-29-11)

We can have no greater task than to be totally at the service of God's plan. And so I would like to encourage and thank all the faithful . . . who feel a responsibility to restore our society's soul. (HM 12-31-11)

It is important to seek to live one's life generously, not according to one's own plan, but to the one God has for each of us, conforming our own will to the Lord's. (HM 11-4-11)

Jesus Christ is the way of perfection, the living and personal synthesis of perfect freedom in total obedience to God's will. (I 40)

Perfection consists in doing the will of God, following the model of the crucified Jesus. (HM 10-23-11)

We have to be ready freely to abandon evil, to raise ourselves from indifference and make room for his word. God respects our freedom. He does not constrain us. He is waiting for us to say "yes," he as it were begs us to say "yes." (HM 9-25-11)

The Christian life must continually measure itself by Christ.... Just as Christ was totally united to the Father and obedient to him, so too the disciples must obey God and be of one mind among themselves. (HM 9-25-11)

It is first and foremost God's primacy that we must recover in our world and in our life, because it is this primacy that enables us to discover the truth of what we are, and it is in knowing and following God's will that we find our own good; giving time and space to God, so that he may be the vital center of our existence. (HM 9-11-11)

It is in this world that we are obliged to resist the delusions of false philosophies and to recognize that we do not live by bread alone, but first and foremost by obedience to God's word. Only when this obedience is put into practice does the attitude develop that is also capable of providing bread for all. (J2 34)

The concept of obedience to God, and so of the right ordering of the earth, is an essential component of the concept of freedom.... The world exists, in other words, because God wanted to create a zone of response to his love, a zone of obedience and freedom. (J2 83)

For the believing Christian, the commandments of the Torah remain a decisive point of reference that he constantly keeps in view; for him the search for God's will in communion with Jesus is above all a signpost for his reason, without which it is always in danger of being dazzled and blinded. (J2 119)

The leap into universality, the new freedom that such a leap requires, is possible only on the basis of a greater obedience. Its power to shape history can come into play only if the authority of the new interpretation is no less than the authority of the original: It must be a divine authority. (J2 120)

The two parts of the great commandment to love God and our neighbor . . . are directions toward the path of love. (J2 134)

God has a will with and for us and it must become the measure of our willing and being; and the essence of "heaven" is that it is where God's will is unswervingly done. (J2 147)

The essence of heaven is oneness with God's will, the oneness of will and truth. Earth becomes "heaven" when and insofar as God's will is done there; and it is merely "earth," the opposite of heaven, when and insofar as it withdraws from the will of God. This is why we pray that it may be on earth as it is in heaven—that earth may become "heaven." (J2 147 & 148)

The Holy Scriptures work on the premise that man has knowledge of God's will in his inmost heart, that anchored deeply within us there is a participation in God's knowing, which we call conscience. (J2 148)

The Son of Man is one person alone, and that person is Jesus. This identity shows us the way, shows us the criterion according to which our lives will one day be judged. (J2 328)

We might also say that our will has to become a filial will. When it does, then we can see . . . it includes what Jesus means by saying that we have to become like children. (J2 343)

The love-story between God and man consists in the very fact that this communion of will increases in a communion of thought and sentiment, and thus our will and God's will increasingly coincide: God's will is no longer for me an alien will, something imposed on me from without by the commandments, but it is now my own will, based on the realization that God is in fact more deeply present to me than I am to myself. (D 10)

Each person finds his good by adherence to God's plan for him, in order to realize it fully—in this plan, he finds his truth, and through adherence to this truth he becomes free (Jn 8:32). To defend the truth, to articulate it with humility and conviction, and to bear witness to it in life are therefore exacting and indispensable forms of charity. (CV 1)

Adhering to the values of Christianity is not merely useful but essential for building a good society and for true integral human development. A Christianity of charity without truth would be more or less interchangeable with a pool of good sentiments, helpful for social cohesion, but of little relevance. (CV 2)

Faith in Christ, communion with Christ's love, is the true fulfillment of all the Law. (J 137)

THE FIFTH JOYFUL MYSTERY
The Finding of Jesus in the Temple

PIETY

*You . . . must be perfect as your heavenly
Father is perfect.* —Matthew 5:48

The Lord wishes to make each one of us a disciple who lives
in personal friendship with him. . . . This is only possible in
the context of a relationship of deep familiarity, imbued with
the warmth of total trust. This is what happens between
friends. (J 69)

He is not only a Teacher but a Friend, indeed, a Brother.
How will we be able to get to know him properly by being
distant? Closeness, familiarity, and habit make us discover
the true identity of Jesus Christ. (J 87)

Holiness does not consist in never having erred or sinned.
Holiness increases the capacity for conversion, for repentance,
for willingness to start again, and, especially, for reconciliation
and forgiveness . . . we can all learn this way of holiness. (J 141)

The moral ideal . . . always consists in realizing a harmoni-
ous integration between word and action, thought and deed,
prayer and dedication to the duties of one's state: this is
the way to realize that synthesis thanks to which the divine
descends to man and man is lifted up until he becomes one
with God. (C 45)

Holiness is always possible, even in difficult times. (C 47)

The monastic life is only a great symbol of baptismal life, of
Christian life. It shows, so to speak, in capital letters what we

write day after day in small letters. It is a prophetic symbol that reveals what the life of the baptized person is, in communion with Christ, with his death and Resurrection. (C 71)

The fundamental, initial, and most simple virtues are particularly important to me: faith, hope, and charity. These are not virtues accessible only to moral heroes; rather they are gifts of God to all the baptized: in them our life develops too.... The whole ascent is present in these virtues. (C 71)

God desires to repose in us, he wishes to renew nature through our conversion, he wants to allow us to share in his divinity. May the Lord help us to make these words the substance of our lives. (C 104)

Faith is not only thought but also touches the whole of our being. Since God became man in flesh and blood, since he entered the tangible world, we must seek and encounter God in all the dimensions of our being. Thus the reality of God, through faith, penetrates our being and transforms it. (C 113 & 114)

Indeed, if we are rightly concerned to care for our physical, human, and intellectual development, it is even more important not to neglect our inner growth, which consists in the knowledge of God, in true knowledge, learned not only from books but from within and in communion with God. (C 143)

The life-style of the Christian who wants to become an authentic disciple of Christ (is) characterized precisely by tenacious adherence to him and by humility, diligence, and the capacity for forgiveness and peace. (C 156)

One arrives at the perfection of spiritual life when the realities of faith are a source of deep joy and real and satisfying

communion with God. One lives only in love and for love.
(C 195)

Christianity, through the Sermon on the Mount, opens up
the high way that is radical in its demands, revealing a new
level of humanity to which men can aspire. (J3 63)

A distinguishing feature of the disciple of Jesus is the fact
that he "lives": beyond the mere fact of existing, he has found
and embraced the *real* life that everyone is seeking. (J3 83)

Holiness, that is to say, belonging to the living God, signifies
mission. (J3 97)

Man becomes true, he becomes himself, when he grows in
God's likeness. Then he attains to his proper nature. (J3 192)

The world listens willingly to teachers when they are also
witnesses. This is a lesson never to be forgotten in the task
of spreading the Gospel: to be a mirror reflecting divine
love, one must first live what one proclaims. (H 10)

The call to holiness is not reserved to the few but is universal.... In all states of life, in accordance with the demands
of each one of them, a possibility of living the Gospel may
be found. In our day, too, each and every Christian must
strive for the "high standard of Christian living." (H 11)

There is only one sorrow in the world: not to be saints,
that is, not to be near to God ... this is the secret of true
happiness: to become saints, close to God! (H 21)

There subsists an intimate and indissoluble relationship
between holiness and joy. (H 21)

The heart of a happy life, of a true life, is friendship with
the Lord Jesus. And this friendship is learned in love for
Sacred Scripture, in love for the liturgy, in profound faith,

in love for Mary, so as to be ever more truly acquainted with God himself and hence with true happiness, which is the goal of our life. (H 121)

The soul passes through the three stages of every path to sanctification: detachment from sin, the practice of the virtues and of love, and sweet and loving union with God. (H 158)

Every genuine evangelizer is always an instrument united with Jesus and with his Church and is fruitful for this very reason. (H 197)

The apostolic ministry is effective and produces fruits of salvation in hearts only if the preacher is a personal witness of Jesus and an instrument at his disposal, bound to him closely by faith in his Gospel and in his Church, by a morally consistent life, and by prayer as ceaseless as love. And this is true for every Christian who wishes to live his adherence to Christ. (H 198)

Holiness, the fullness of the Christian life, does not consist in carrying out extraordinary enterprises but in being united with Christ, in living his mysteries, in making our own his example, his thoughts, his behavior. (H 239)

The measure of holiness stems from the stature that Christ achieves in us, in as much as with the power of the Holy Spirit, we model our whole life on his. It is being conformed to Jesus. (H 239)

A holy life is not primarily the result of our efforts, of our actions, because it is God, the three times Holy (Is 6:3), who sanctifies us, it is the Holy Spirit's action that enlivens us from within, it is the very life of the Risen Christ that is communicated to us and that transforms us. (H 240)

We are all called to holiness: it is the very measure of Christian living. (H 243)

Holiness is not confined by cultural, social, political or religious barriers. Its language, that of love and truth, is understandable to all people of good will and it draws them to Jesus Christ, the inexhaustible source of new life. (HM 10-7-12)

Someone can stand near the tabernacle and, at the same time, be far from the living God. What matters is inner closeness! God came so close to us that he himself became a man: this should disconcert and surprise us again and again! He is so close that he is one of us. (HM 9-2-12)

Stay firm in the faith, rooted in Christ through the Word and the Eucharist; be people who pray, in order to remain linked for ever to Christ, like branches to the vine. (HM 7-15-12)

Renew your commitment and rekindle the feelings that inspired and continue to inspire the gift of yourselves to the Lord. Let us do this today, this is the commitment you are called to realize every day of your life. (HM 2-2-12)

Be holy! Make Christ the center of your lives! Build the edifice of your existence on him! In Jesus you will find the strength to open yourselves to others and to make yourselves, after his example, a gift for the whole of humanity. (HM 5-8-11)

I wish not merely to be called Christian, but also to be Christian, said Saint Ignatius of Antioch ... let us pray that, increasingly, we may not only be called Christian but may actually be such. (HM 4-21-11)

Christians are a priestly people for the world. Christians should make the living God visible to the world, they should bear witness to him and lead people toward him. (HM 4-21-11)

We must see to it that the beauty and contemporary relevance of the faith is rediscovered, not as an isolated event, affecting some particular moment in our lives, but as a constant orientation, affecting even the simplest choices, establishing a profound unity within the person, so that he becomes just, hard-working, generous and good. (HM 12-31-11)

(Do) not only receive the sacraments but live them out, in order to be true Christians. This aim, *to receive,* must be *to live* ... justice must sprout, just as the seed sprouts from the ground. Live the sacraments so that justice, law and love will sprout likewise. (HM 12-11-11)

It is not words that matter, but deeds, deeds of conversion and faith....We have to be saints so as not to create a contradiction between the sign that we are and the reality that we wish to signify. (HM 9-25-11; 8-21-11)

God's things deserve haste, indeed, the only things in the world that deserve haste are precisely those of God, which are truly urgent for our life. (HM 8-15-11)

If we had to choose today, would Jesus of Nazareth, the son of Mary, the Son of the Father, have a chance? Do we really know Jesus at all? Do we understand him? Do we not perhaps have to make an effort, today as always, to get to know him all over again? (J2 41)

Blessed is the man who trusts in the Lord. These are the words of promise. At the same time, though, they are criteria for the discernment of spirits and so they prove to be directions for finding the right path. (J2 71)

The disciple is bound to the mystery of Christ. His life is immersed in communion with Christ: "It is no longer I who live, but Christ who lives in me" (Gal 2:20). The Beatitudes are the transposition of Cross and Resurrection into discipleship. But they apply to the disciple because they were first paradigmatically lived by Christ himself. (J2 74)

The Sermon on the Mount ... draws a comprehensive portrait of the right way to live. It aims to show us how to be a human being. We could sum up its fundamental insights by saying that man can be understood only in light of God, and that his life is made righteous only when he lives it in relation to God. (J2 128)

A living relationship with Christ is decisive if we are to keep on the right path.... Jesus must truly be the center of our life. (D 20 & C 138)

Life in its true sense is not something we have exclusively in or from ourselves: it is a relationship. And life in its totality is a relationship with him who is the source of life. If we are in relation with him who does not die, who is Life itself and Love itself, then we are in life. Then we "live." (S 14)

Knowledge is never purely the work of the intellect ... if it aspires to be wisdom capable of directing man in the light of his first beginnings and his final end, it must be "seasoned" with the "salt" of charity. Deeds without knowledge are blind, and knowledge without love is sterile. (CV 15)

Development requires attention to the spiritual life, a serious consideration of the experiences of trust in God, spiritual fellowship in Christ, reliance upon God's providence and mercy, love and forgiveness, self-denial, acceptance of others, justice and peace. All this is essential if "hearts of stone" are to be transformed into "hearts of flesh" (Ezek 36:26). (CV 42)

The one true Teacher, Jesus, dwells in the heart of every believer and wants to take total possession of it. (H 124)

THE SORROWFUL
MYSTERIES

THE FIRST SORROWFUL MYSTERY
The Agony in the Garden

SORROW FOR SIN

*The cares of the world, and the delight in riches, and
the desire for other things, enter in and choke the
word, and it proves unfruitful.* —Mark 4:19

Wherever communion with God, which is communion
with the Father, the Son, and the Holy Spirit, is destroyed,
the root and source of our communion with one another
are destroyed. And wherever we do not live communion
among ourselves, communion with the Trinitarian God is
not alive and true either. (J 18)

The most important thing is never to distance oneself from
Jesus.... Thus, Christian life is defined as a life with Jesus
Christ, a life to spend together with him (J 92)

The Prodigal Son's awareness of his sin enabled him to start
out on the path of return and thereby to experience the joy
of reconciliation with the Father. Human limitations and
fragility are not an obstacle, on condition that they help to
make us ever more aware that we need Christ's redeeming
love. (I 34 & 35)

The three fundamental temptations of every human being
(are) the temptation of self-affirmation and the desire to put

oneself at the center, the temptation of sensuality, and, lastly,
the temptation of anger and revenge. (c 21)

We think of values that are justly defended today, such as
tolerance, freedom and dialogue. But a tolerance that no
longer distinguishes between good and evil would become
chaotic and self-destructive, just as a freedom that did not
respect the freedom of others or find the common measure
of our respective liberties would become anarchy and destroy
authority. (c 65)

The primacy of one's own will destroys the social fabric
and the peace of souls ... All too often culture seems to be
marked by a growing tendency to ethical relativism; the
self alone decides what is good for it, for oneself, at this
moment. (c 110 & 172)

God is love. But love can also be hated when it challenges
us to transcend ourselves. It is not a romantic "good feel-
ing." Redemption is not "wellness"... it is a liberation from
imprisonment in self-absorption. (j1 86)

Violence does not build up the kingdom of God, the kingdom of humanity. On the contrary, it is a favorite instrument
of the Antichrist, however idealistic its religious motivation
may be. It serves, not humanity, but inhumanity. (j3 15)

Is it not the case that our need to be reconciled with God—
the silent, mysterious, seemingly absent, and yet omnipresent
God—is the real problem of the whole of world history?
(j3 79)

God cannot simply ignore man's disobedience and all the
evil of history; he cannot treat it as if it were inconsequential
or meaningless.... The fact that God now confronts evil
himself, because men are incapable of doing so—therein lies

the "unconditional" goodness of God, which can never be opposed to truth or the justice that goes with it. (J3 132 & 133)

Drowsiness deadens the soul, so that it remains undisturbed by the power of the Evil One at work in the world and by all the injustice and suffering ravaging the earth. In its stage of numbness, the soul prefers not to see all this; it is easily persuaded that things cannot be so bad, so as to continue in the self-satisfaction of its own comfortable existence. (J3 153)

In Jesus, it is man himself that is manifested. In him is displayed the suffering of all who are subjected to violence, all the downtrodden. His suffering mirrors the inhumanity of worldly power, which so ruthlessly crushes the powerless. In him is reflected what we call "sin": this is what happens when man turns his back upon God and takes control over the world into his own hands. (J3 199)

Ignorance diminishes guilt, and it leaves open the path to conversion. But it does not simply excuse, because at the same time it reveals a deadening of the heart that resists the call of Truth. (J3 208)

Absolutizing what is not absolute but relative is called totalitarianism. It does not liberate man, but takes away his dignity and enslaves him. (G 54)

Free time is empty if God is not present ... our initial impression is that having to include time for Mass on Sunday is rather inconvenient. But if you make the effort, you will realize that this is what gives a proper focus to your free time. (G 60)

The holiness of God (is) no longer recognized, and, consequently, contempt (is) shown for the sacredness of human life. (G 70)

Terrorism of any kind is a perverse and cruel choice which shows contempt for the sacred right to life and undermines the very foundations of all civil coexistence. (G 75)

We know that secularism and dechristianization are gaining ground, that relativism is growing and that the influence of Catholic ethics and morals is in constant decline. Many people abandon the Church or, if they stay, accept only a part of Catholic teaching, picking and choosing between only certain aspects of Christianity. (G 94)

In the human being the idea of absolute freedom, placed in the will, forgetting the connection with the truth, does not know that freedom itself must be liberated from the limits imposed on it by sin. (H 92)

Modern history actually teaches us that freedom is authentic and helps with building a truly human civilization only when it is reconciled with truth. If freedom is detached from truth, it becomes, tragically, a principle of the destruction of man's inner harmony, a source of the abuse of power by the strongest and the violent and a cause of suffering and sorrow. (H 92)

A true renewal of the ecclesial community is obtained with a sincere spirit of repentance and a demanding process of conversion, rather than with a change of structures. This is a message that we should never forget. (H 100 & 101)

Today we all risk living as though God did not exist. (H 128)

Guard against the temptations of the devil, who often conceals himself behind deceptive guises, later to sow doubts about faith, vocational uncertainty, and sensuality. (H 168)

In our own day, lots of people are ready to "rend their clothing" in the face of scandals and acts of injustice — the fault naturally of others—but few seem prepared to do something about their own "hearts," their own consciences and their own intentions, allowing the Lord to transform, renew and convert them. (HM 2-13-13)

The light of faith has grown dim and people have drifted away from God, no longer considering him relevant for their lives. These people have therefore lost a precious treasure, they have "fallen" from a lofty dignity—not financially or in terms of earthly power, but in a Christian sense—their lives have lost secure and sound direction and they have become, often unconsciously, beggars for the meaning of existence. (HM 10-28-12)

A world which distances itself from God does not become better but worse. (HM 8-15-12)

God wants to give us himself and his Word. He knows that in distancing ourselves from him we will soon run into difficulty—like the Prodigal Son of the parable—and, especially, that we will lose our human dignity. And for this reason he assures us that he is infinite mercy. (HM 1-8-12)

In the world there is evil, there is selfishness, there is wickedness, and God could come to judge this world, to destroy evil, to punish those who work in darkness. Instead, he shows his love for the world and for men and women, despite their sin, and sends what is most precious to him: his Only-Begotten Son. (HM 6-19-11)

Love is (being) reduced to sentimental emotion and to the gratification of instinctive impulses, without a commitment to build lasting bonds of reciprocal belonging and without openness to life. We are called to oppose such a mentality! (HM 6-5-11)

If our relationship with God is disturbed, if the fundamental orientation to our being is awry, we cannot be truly healed in body and soul. (HM 4-21-11)

It is in God that our last hour must come to a close, the last hour of time and history. To overlook this goal of our lives would be to fall into the void, to live without meaning. (HM 12-31-11)

Many are those whose faith is weak, whose way of thinking, habits and lifestyle do not know the reality of the Gospel, and who think that seeking selfish satisfaction, easy gain or power is the ultimate goal of human life. (HM 11-20-11)

A society which forgets God, excludes God, precisely in order to have life, falls into a culture of death....What seems to be a culture of life becomes the anticulture of death, where God is absent. (I 71)

We are glad and thankful for the gift of freedom. However, when we see the terrible things that happen as a result of it, we are frightened. Let us put our trust in God, whose power manifests itself above all in mercy and forgiveness. (HM 9-25-11)

Only in openness to God, in receiving his gift, do we become truly free, free from the slavery of sin that disfigures man's face, and capable of serving the true good of our brethren. (HM 9-11-11)

History shows us, dramatically, that the objective of guaranteeing everyone development, material well-being and peace, by leaving out God and his revelation, has been resolved by giving people stones instead of bread. (HM 9-11-11)

At the heart of all temptations is the act of pushing God aside because we perceive him as secondary, if not actually superfluous and annoying, in comparison with all the apparently far more urgent matters that fill our lives. (J2 28)

Only the man who is reconciled with God can also be reconciled and in harmony with himself, and only the man who is reconciled with God and with himself can establish peace around him and throughout the world. (J2 85)

When men lose sight of God, peace disintegrates and violence proliferates to a formerly unimaginable degree of cruelty. This we see only too clearly today.... The loss of God and neighbor (is) the path to ruin. (J2 85 & 96)

It is only when you have lost God that you have lost yourself. (J2 166)

We get rid of God; there is no measuring rod above us; we ourselves are our only measure....What happens to man and the world next? We are already beginning to see it. (J2 257)

One does not make the world more human by refusing to act humanly here and now. We contribute to a better world only by personally doing good now, with full commitment and wherever we have the opportunity. (D 18)

Sin is understood by the Fathers as the destruction of the unity of the human race, as fragmentation and division. Babel, the place where languages were confused, the place of separation, is seen to be an expression of what sin fundamentally is. (S 8)

Suffering stems partly from our finitude, and partly from the mass of sin which has accumulated over the course of history, and continues to grow unabated today. (S 18)

For the great majority of people there remains in the depths of their being an ultimate interior openness to truth, to love, to God. In the concrete choices of life, however, it is covered over by every new compromise with evil. (s 23)

When the State promotes, teaches, or actually imposes forms of practical atheism, it deprives its citizens of the moral and spiritual strength that is indispensable for attaining integral human development and it impedes them from moving forward. (CV 15)

It sometimes happens that economically developed countries export this reductive vision of the person and his destiny to poor countries. This is the damage that "superdevelopment" causes to authentic development when it is accompanied by "moral underdevelopment." (CV 15)

Sometimes modern man is wrongly convinced that he is the sole author of himself, his life and society. This is a presumption that follows from being selfishly closed in upon himself, and it is a consequence — to express it in faith terms — of *original sin.* (CV 17)

Ideological rejection of God and an atheism of indifference, oblivious to the Creator and at risk of becoming equally oblivious to human values, constitute some of the chief obstacles to development today. A humanism which excludes God is an inhuman humanism. (CV 41)

I urge you to receive the Sacrament of Reconciliation regularly. (HM 12-16-12)

THE SECOND SORROWFUL MYSTERY
The Scourging at the Pillar

PURITY

Clean the inside of cup and dish first so that the
outside may become clean as well. —Matthew 23:26

What counts is to place Jesus Christ at the center of our lives, so that our identity is marked essentially by the encounter, by communion with Christ and with his Word. In his light every other value is recovered and purified. (J 111)

It is to (God) and his grace alone that we owe what we are as Christians. Since nothing and no one can replace him, it is necessary that we pay homage to nothing and no one else but him. No idol should pollute our spiritual universe, or otherwise, instead of enjoying the freedom acquired, we will relapse into a humiliating form of slavery. (J 117)

The passions are not evil in themselves; they become so through human freedom's wrong use of them. If they are purified, the passions reveal to man the path toward God with energy unified by ascesis and grace. (C 69)

The words of Sacred Scripture purify our somewhat blind reason and help us to recover the memory of what we, as the image of God, carry in our hearts, unfortunately wounded by sin. (C 120)

The gift of purity is an act of God. Man cannot make himself fit for God, whatever systems of purification he may follow.... It is the God who comes down to us who makes us clean. Purity is a gift. (J3 61)

The Lord stands before us as the servant of God—he who for our sake became one who serves, who carries our burden and so grants us true purity, the capacity to draw close to God. (J3 74)

Central to the Christian life are both the sacrament of Baptism, by which we are taken up into Christ's obedience, and also the Eucharist, in which the Lord's obedience on the Cross embraces us all, purifies us, and draws us into the perfect worship offered by Jesus Christ. (J3 235)

We all know that we are imperfect, that we are unable to be a fitting house for him. Let us therefore begin Holy Mass by meditating and praying to him, so that he will take from us what divides us from him and what separates us from each other. (G 56)

Let us never forget this teaching: the holiness of the Eucharist appeals to us to be pure, to live in a way that is consistent with the mystery we celebrate. (H 21)

Think of the true riches, those of the heart, which make people good and merciful and permit them to lay up treasure in Heaven. (H 33)

Learn at the school of the divine Teacher: let us listen to his word of life and truth that resonates in the depths of our soul. Let us purify our thoughts and actions so that he may dwell within us and that we may understand his divine voice, which draws us toward true happiness. (H 49)

Grace, lavished upon us by God and communicated through the mystery of the Incarnate Word, is an absolutely free gift with which nature is healed, strengthened, and assisted in pursuing the innate desire for happiness in the heart of every man and of every woman. (H 75)

Monastic life (is) an eloquent testimony of God's primacy and an appeal to all to walk toward holiness, free from any compromise with evil. (c 140)

Knowledge of God comes, not from books, but rather from spiritual experience, from spiritual life. Knowledge of God is born from a process of inner purification that begins with conversion of heart through the power of faith and love. It passes through profound repentance and sincere sorrow for one's sins to attain union with Christ, the source of joy and peace. (c 143)

(Let us) pay attention to our spiritual life, to the hidden presence of God within us, to the sincerity of the conscience and to purification, to conversion of heart, so that the Holy Spirit may really become present in us and guide us. (c 143)

The sacraments are the great treasure of the Church, and it is the task of each one of us to celebrate them with spiritual profit. In them an ever-amazing event touches our lives: Christ, through the visible signs, comes to us, purifies us, transforms us, and makes us share in his divine friendship. (c 215)

Jesus's love "to the end" is what cleanses us, washes us. The gesture of washing feet expresses precisely this: it is the servant-love of Jesus that draws us out of our pride and makes us fit for God, makes us "clean." (J3 57)

"You are clean, but not all of you," the Lord says. This sentence reveals the great gift of purification that he offers to us, because he wants to be at table together with us, to become our food. (I 34)

If man is to enter God's presence, to have fellowship with God, he must be "clean." Yet the more he moves into the light, the more he senses how defiled he is, how much he stands in need of cleansing. (J3 57)

We see the radical transformation that Jesus brought to the concept of purity before God: it is not ritual actions that make us pure. Purity and impurity arise within man's heart and depend on the condition of his heart (Mk 7:14-23). (J3 58)

Faith cleanses the heart. It is the result of God's initiative toward man. It is not simply a choice that men make for themselves. Faith comes about because men are touched deep within by God's Spirit, who opens and purifies their hearts. (J3 58 & 59)

Rubbish is not only on some streets of the world. There is also rubbish in our consciences and in our souls. Only the light of the Lord, his strength and his love, cleanses us, purifies us, showing us the right path. (H 146 & 147)

Love for God itself becomes a flame; love itself cleanses (the soul) from the residue of sin. (H 176)

When God purifies man, he binds him with the finest golden thread, that is, his love, and draws him toward himself with such strong affection that man is, as it were, "overcome and won over and completely beside himself." Thus man's heart is pervaded by God's love, which becomes the one guide, the one driving force of his life. (H 176 & 177)

Virginity of soul is the *state of grace,* a supreme value.... It is a gift of God which is to be received and preserved with humility and trust. (H 183)

Human endeavor on its own is unable to reach the profound roots of the person's bad inclinations and habits: all it can do is to check them but it cannot entirely uproot them. This requires the special action of God, which radically purifies the spirit and prepares it for the union of love with him. (H 203)

The growth of faith, hope, and charity keeps pace with the work of purification and with the gradual union with God until they are transformed in him. When it reaches this goal, the soul is immersed in Trinitarian life itself. (H 204)

Man finds himself betwixt this twofold gravitational force; everything depends on our escaping the gravitational field of evil and becoming free to be attracted completely by the gravitational force of God, which makes us authentic, elevates us and grants us true freedom. (HM 4-17-11)

We are striving for pure hearts and clean hands, we are seeking truth, we are seeking the face of God. Let us show the Lord that we desire to be righteous, and let us ask him: Draw us upwards! Make us pure! (HM 4-17-11)

God wants to take the dead heart of stone out of our breast and give us a living heart of flesh (Ez 36:26), a loving heart, a heart of gentleness and peace. He wants to bestow new life upon us, full of vitality. (HM 9-22-11)

(Jesus Christ) takes upon himself all our sins, anxieties and sufferings and he purifies and transforms us, in a way that is ultimately mysterious, into good branches that produce good wine. (HM 9-22-11)

Once sin has been overcome and man's harmony with God restored, creation is reconciled, too. Creation, torn asunder by strife, once more becomes the dwelling place of peace, as Paul expresses it when he speaks of the groaning of creation, which "waits with eager longing for the revealing of the sons of God" (Rom 8:19). (J2 27)

If man's heart is not good, then nothing else can turn out good, either. And the goodness of the human heart can ultimately come only from the One who is goodness, who is Good itself. (J2 34)

The organ for seeing God is the heart. The intellect alone is not enough. In order for man to become capable of perceiving God, the energies of his existence have to work in harmony. His will must be pure and so too must the underlying affective dimension of his soul, which gives intelligence and will their direction. (J2 92 & 93)

Man can experience authentic happiness only within his own interiority.... The heart—the wholeness of man—must be pure, interiorly open and free, in order for man to be able to see God. (C 14 & J2 93)

The pure heart is the loving heart that enters into communion of service and obedience with Jesus Christ. Love is the fire that purifies and unifies intellect, will, and emotion, thereby making man one with himself, inasmuch as it makes him one in God's eyes. (J2 95 & 96)

Prayer is really all about ... God's desire to offer us the gift of himself—that is the gift of all gifts, the "one thing necessary." Prayer is a way of gradually purifying and correcting our wishes and of slowly coming to realize what we really need: God and his Spirit. (J2 137)

How do I treat God's holy name? Do I stand in reverence before the mystery of the burning bush, before his incomprehensible closeness, even to the point of his presence in the Eucharist, where he truly gives himself entirely into our hands? Do I take care that God's holy companionship with us will draw us up into his purity and sanctity? (J2 145)

The Lord's gift of faith restores the pure breath of life: the breath of the Creator, the breath of the Holy Spirit, which alone can give health to the world. (J2 175)

The promised river of life that decontaminates the briny soil and allows the fullness of life to ripen and bear fruit really does exist. It is he who, in "loving to the end," endured the Cross and now lives with a life that can never again be threatened by death. It is the living Christ. (J2 247)

The Church and the individual need constant purification. Processes of purification, which are as necessary as they are painful, run through the whole of history, the whole life of those who have dedicated themselves to Christ. The mystery of death and resurrection is ever present in these purifications. (J2 260)

If reason is to be exercised properly, it must undergo constant purification, since it can never be completely free of the danger of a certain ethical blindness. (D 15)

There can be people who are utterly pure, completely permeated by God, and thus fully open to their neighbors — people for whom communion with God even now gives direction to their entire being and whose journey towards God only brings to fulfillment what they already are. (S 23)

The way we live our lives is not immaterial, but our defilement does not stain us forever if we have at least continued to reach out towards Christ, towards truth and towards love. Indeed, it has already been burned away through Christ's Passion. (S 24)

The ascent to God occurs precisely in the descent of humble service, in the descent of love, for love is God's essence, and is thus the power that truly purifies man and enables him to perceive God and to see him. In Jesus Christ, God has revealed himself in his descending. (J2 95)

Just as the stronger the fire burns and consumes wood, the brighter it grows until it blazes into a flame, so the Holy Spirit, who purifies and "cleanses" the soul during the dark night, with time illuminates and warms it as though it were a flame. (H 202)

The long and difficult process of purification demands a personal effort, but the real protagonist is God: all that the human being can do is to "prepare" himself, to be open to divine action, and not to set up obstacles to it. (H 204)

To pray is not to step outside history and withdraw to our own private corner of happiness. When we pray properly we undergo a process of inner purification which opens us up to God and thus to our fellow human beings as well. (S 17)

THE THIRD SORROWFUL MYSTERY
The Crowning of Thorns

COURAGE

Courage! It is I! Do not be afraid. —Matthew 14:27

It is the Lord who says to me, who says to you: Follow me! And we must have the courage and humility to follow Jesus, because he is the Way, the Truth, and the Life. (J 43)

Our identity requires strength, clarity, and courage in light of the contradictions of the world in which we live. (J 103)

Our radical belonging to Christ and the fact that "we are in him" must imbue in us an attitude of total trust and immense joy. In short, we must indeed exclaim with Saint Paul: "If God is for us, who is against us?" (Rom 8:31). (J 117)

Our Christian life stands on the soundest and safest rock one can imagine. And from it we draw all our energy, precisely as the Apostle wrote: "I can do all things in him who strengthens me" (Phil 4:13). (J 117)

Charitable social commitment must never be separated from the courageous proclamation of the faith . . . charity and the proclamation of the faith always go hand in hand. (J 138)

What does the Lord want of me? Of course, this is always a great adventure, but life can be successful only if we have the courage to be adventurous, trusting that the Lord will never leave me alone, that the Lord will go with me and help me. (I 29)

The good is always infinitely greater than the vast mass of evil, however terrible it may be. (J3 231)

Vigilance means first of all openness to the good, to the truth, to God, in the midst of an often meaningless world and in the midst of the power of evil. (J3 288)

I encourage you to commit yourselves without reserve to serving Christ, whatever the cost. The encounter with Jesus Christ will allow you to experience in your hearts the joy of his living and life-giving presence and enable you to bear witness to it before others. (G 39)

Century after century, we also see the birth of forces of reform and renewal, because God's newness is inexhaustible and provides ever new strength to forge ahead. (H 7)

Take heart, even in the night of faith, even amidst our many doubts, do not let go of the Lord's hand, walk hand in hand with him, believe in God's goodness. This is how to follow the right path! (H 171)

The journey with Christ, traveling with Christ, "the Way," is not an additional burden in our life, it is not something that would make our burden even heavier, but something quite different. It is a light, a power that helps us to bear it. (H 205)

If a person bears great love in himself, this love gives him wings, as it were, and he can face all life's troubles more easily because he carries in himself this great light. (H 205)

The new evangelization stands in need of well-trained apostles, zealous and courageous, so that the light and beauty of the Gospel may prevail over the cultural tendencies of ethical relativism and religious indifference and transform the various ways of thinking and acting into genuine Christian humanism. (H 221)

We know that at the moment of deep suffering, at the moment of the ultimate loneliness of death, no insurance policy will be able to protect us. The only valid insurance in those moments is the one that comes to us from the Lord, who also assures us: "Do not fear, I am always with you." We can fall, but in the end we fall into God's hands, and God's hands are good hands. (I 19)

Let us not be afraid to aim high, for God's heights; let us not be afraid that God will ask too much of us, but let ourselves be guided by his Word in every daily action, even when we feel poor, inadequate, sinners. It will be he who transforms us in accordance with his love. (H 243)

The courage to stand firm in the truth is unavoidably demanded of those whom the Lord sends like sheep among wolves. "Those who fear the Lord will not be timid," says the Book of Sirach (34:16). (HM 1-6-13)

The fear of God frees us from the fear of men. It liberates. (HM 1-6-13)

Our criterion is the Lord himself. If we defend his cause, we will constantly gain others to the way of the Gospel. (HM 1-6-13)

There is no longer any reason for distrust, discouragement, sorrow, whatever the situation that must be faced, because we are certain of the Lord's presence which alone suffices to calm and cheer hearts. (HM 12-16-12)

There is no doubt that the Lord, the Good Shepherd, will abundantly bless these efforts which proceed from zeal for his Person and his Gospel. (HM 10-28-12)

A desire for God makes us tireless pilgrims, nourishing in us the courage and the power of faith, which at the same time is the courage and the power of love. (HM 8-15-12)

The Resurrection of Jesus Christ confirms that God's goodness conquers evil and love conquers death. He accompanies us in the fight against the destructive power of sin that damages humanity and God's entire creation. (HM 1-25-12)

We know that we are not alone and that our witness is sustained by the Holy Spirit. (HM 1-8-12)

Be confident: the Risen Lord is walking with you, yesterday, today and forever. (HM 5-8-11)

Reason is stronger than unreason, truth stronger than lies, and love is stronger than death. (HM 4-23-11)

We do not need a generic, indefinite god but rather the living, true God who unfolds the horizon of man's future to a prospect of firm, well-founded hope, a hope rich in eternity that enables us to face the present courageously in all its aspects. (HM 12-15-11)

Christ has overcome death and he brings us with him in his resurrection. (HM 11-20-11)

Christ's death is the source of life, for into it God poured all of his love, as in an immense cascade.... The abyss of death is filled by another abyss that is greater still, namely, the love of God, which is such that death no longer has power over Jesus Christ (Rom 8:9), nor over those who are associated with him through faith and baptism. (HM 11-3-11)

To you, lay faithful, young people and families, I say: do not be afraid to live and to witness to faith in the different sectors of society, in the many contexts of human life! You have every reason to show that you are strong, confident and courageous, and this is thanks to the light of faith and the power of love. (HM 10-9-11)

It is ultimately at Jesus that the persecution of his Church is directed . . . when we are oppressed for the sake of the faith, we are not alone: Jesus Christ is beside us and with us. (HM 9-22-11)

The image of the vine is a sign of hope and confidence. Christ himself came into this world through his incarnation, to be our root. Whatever hardship or drought befall us, he is the source that offers the water of life, that feeds and strengthens us. (HM 9-22-11)

The risen Lord gives us a place of refuge, a place of light, hope and confidence, a place of rest and security. When drought and death loom over the branches, then in Christ we find future life and joy. In him we always find forgiveness and the opportunity to begin again, to be transformed as we are drawn into his love. (HM 9-22-11)

Every time has its own challenges; but in every age God gives the right grace to face and overcome those challenges with love and realism. (HM 8-21-11)

When man allows himself to be enlightened by the splendor of truth, he inwardly becomes a courageous peacemaker. (I 58)

God's dwelling place necessarily means a special place of divine protection. (J2 35)

You will never lose a final refuge. You know that the foundation of the world is love, so that even when no human being can or will help you, you may go on, trusting in the One who loves you . . . we cultivate (this trust) on the authority of Scripture and at the invitation of the risen Lord. (J2 38)

God's power works quietly in this world, but it is the true and lasting power. Again and again, God's cause seems to be in its death throes. Yet over and over again it proves to be the thing that truly endures and saves. (J2 44)

We cannot ignore the people who trust so totally in God that they seek no security other than him. They encourage us to trust God—to count on him amid life's great challenges. (J2 152)

Once we have asked for and obtained protection against evil, we are safely sheltered against everything the devil and the world can contrive. What could the world make you fear if you are protected in the world by God himself? (J2 166)

Faith, which sees the love of God revealed in the pierced heart of Jesus on the Cross, gives rise to love. Love is the light—and in the end, the only light—that can always illuminate a world grown dim and gives us the courage needed to keep living and working. (D 21)

The human being needs unconditional love. He needs the certainty which makes him say: "neither death, nor life, nor angels, nor principalities, nor things present, nor things to come, nor powers, nor height, nor depth, nor anything else in all creation, will be able to separate us from the love of God in Christ Jesus our Lord" (Rom 8:38-39). . . . This is what it means to say: Jesus Christ has "redeemed" us. (S 14)

Only the great certitude of hope that my own life and history in general, despite all failures, are held firm by the indestructible power of Love, and that this gives them their meaning and importance, only this kind of hope can then give the courage to act and to persevere. (S 17 & 18)

THE FOURTH SORROWFUL MYSTERY
The Carrying of the Cross

PATIENCE

(A)s for the (seeds) in the good soil, they are those who,
hearing the word, hold it fast in an honest and good
heart, and bring forth fruit with patience. —Luke 8:15

The school of faith is not a triumphal march but a journey marked daily by suffering and love, trials and faithfulness. (J 46)

The journey, not only exterior but above all interior, from the mount of the Transfiguration to the mount of the Agony, symbolizes the entire pilgrimage of Christian life.... In following Jesus we know that even in difficulties we are on the right path. (J 62)

Learning to love is a long and demanding process. (C 193)

Abasement and exaltation are mysteriously intertwined.... All through history, people look upon the disfigured face of Jesus, and there they recognize the glory of God. (J3 182)

Jesus in the throes of his Passion is an image of hope: God is on the side of those who suffer. (J3 200)

Man becomes free when he binds himself, when he finds roots, for it is then that he can grow and mature. We must teach patience, discernment, realism, but without false compromises, so as not to water down the Gospel! (G 96)

In the life of the saints there is no contradiction between prophetic charism and the charism of governance, and if tension arises, they know to await patiently the times determined by the Holy Spirit. (H 16)

To have confirmation that an inspiration comes from God, it is always necessary to be immersed in prayer, to wait patiently, to seek friendship and exchanges with other good souls, and to submit all things to the judgment of the Pastors of the Church. (H 150)

To increase their faith, the Lord often asks Saints to sustain trials. (H 150)

The gradual purification of the soul (is) necessary in order to scale the peaks of Christian perfection. (H 202)

As we gradually proceed on our journey of faith, we realize that Jesus exercises on us the liberating action of God's love which brings us out of our selfishness, our withdrawal into ourselves, to lead us to a full life in communion with God and open to others. (HM 1-13-13)

In the dominant culture today, the idea of victory is often associated with instant success. In the Christian perspective, on the contrary, victory is a long, and in our human eyes, not always uncomplicated process of transformation and growth in goodness. It happens in accordance with God's time, not ours. (HM 1-25-12)

There is nothing magic about Christianity. There are no short-cuts; everything passes through the humble and patient logic of the grain of wheat that broke open to give life, the logic of faith that moves mountains with the gentle power of God. (HM 6-23-11)

The Apostle's exhortation to patient perseverance, which in our time might leave us somewhat perplexed, is in fact the way to accept the question of God in depth, the meaning he has in life and in history, because it is actually by patience, fidelity and constancy in seeking God and openness to him that he reveals his Face. (HM 12-25-11)

Patience is a virtue of those who entrust themselves to this presence (of God) in history, who do not allow themselves to succumb to the temptation to put all their hope in the immediate, in a purely horizontal perspective. (HM 12-15-11)

He is the patient and faithful God, who knows how to wait and how to respect our freedom. (HM 12-15-11)

In Christ there is everything, fullness; we need time to make one of the dimensions of his mystery our own. We could say that this is a journey of transformation in which the mystery of Christ's resurrection is brought about and made manifest in us. (HM 10-23-11)

That courageous witness, that patient life with God, that patient trust in God's guidance are like a precious seed that promises rich fruit for the future. (HM 9-24-11)

Christ can transform into love even the burdensome and oppressive aspects of our lives. It is important that we "abide" in Christ, in the vine. (HM 9-22-11)

When man begins to see and to live from God's perspective, when he is a companion on Jesus's way, then he lives by new standards, and something of the *éschaton*, of the reality to come, is already present. Jesus brings joy into the midst of affliction. (J2 72)

The more we can bear pain, the more we will be able to understand others and open ourselves to them. (J2 130)

God does not abandon man, but he does allow him to be tried. (J2 162)

Initial enthusiasm is easy. Afterward, though, it is time to stand firm, even along the monotonous desert paths that we are called upon to traverse in this life—with the patience it takes to tread evenly, a patience in which the romanticism of the initial awakening subsides, so that only the deep, pure Yes of faith remains. This is the way to produce good wine. (J2 262)

There are times when the burden of need and our own limitations might tempt us to become discouraged. But precisely then we are helped by the knowledge that, in the end, we are only instruments in the Lord's hands; and this knowledge frees us from the presumption of thinking that we alone are personally responsible for building a better world. (D 20)

Often we cannot understand why God refrains from intervening. Yet he does not prevent us from crying out, like Jesus on the Cross: "My God, my God, why have you forsaken me?" (Mt 27:46). We should continue asking this question in prayerful dialogue before his face: "Lord, holy and true, how long will it be?" (Rev 6:10). (D 21)

For the believer, it is impossible to imagine that God is powerless or that "perhaps he is asleep" (1 Kg 18:27). Instead, our crying out is, as it was for Jesus on the Cross, the deepest and most radical way of affirming our faith in his sovereign power. (D 21)

Knowing how to wait, while patiently enduring trials, is necessary for the believer to be able "to receive what is promised." In the religious context of ancient Judaism, this word was used expressly for the expectation of God which was characteristic of Israel, for their persevering faithfulness to God on the basis of the certainty of the Covenant in a world which contradicts God. (S 6)

What does it mean to "offer something up"? Those who did so were convinced that they could insert these little annoyances into Christ's great "com-passion" so that they somehow became part of the treasury of compassion so greatly needed by the human race.... Maybe we should consider whether it might be judicious to revive this practice ourselves. (S 20)

Speculation over history, looking ahead into the unknown future—these are not fitting attitudes for a disciple. Christianity is the present: it is both gift and task, receiving the gift of God's inner closeness and—as a consequence—bearing witness to Jesus Christ. (J3 282)

The soul's darkness is gradually illuminated by walking with Jesus. (J3 203)

In order to mature, in order to make real progress on the path leading from a superficial piety into profound oneness with God's will, man needs to be tried. Just as the juice of the grape has to ferment in order to become a fine wine, so too man needs purifications and transformations. (J2 162)

Purification and fruit belong together; only by undergoing God's purifications can we bear the fruit that flows into the eucharistic mystery and so leads to the marriage feast that is the goal toward which God directs history. (J2 262)

The triumph of love will be the last word of world history. Vigilance is demanded of Christians as the basic attitude for the "interim time." (J3 287)

St. James' invitation: "be patient, therefore, brethren, until the coming of the Lord," reminds us that the certainty of the world's great hope is given to us, that *we are not alone* and that we do not build history *by ourselves.* (HM 12-15-11)

Faith tells us that God has given his Son for our sakes and gives us the victorious certainty that it is really true: God is love! It thus transforms our impatience and our doubts into the sure hope that God holds the world in his hands.... In spite of all darkness he ultimately triumphs in glory. (D 21)

Even Mary's faith is a "journeying" faith, a faith that is repeatedly shrouded in darkness and has to mature by persevering through the darkness. (J1 125)

Since faith involves following the Master, it must become constantly stronger, deeper and more mature, to the extent that it leads to a closer and more intense relationship with Jesus. (HM 8-21-11)

Hope is practiced through the virtue of patience, which continues to do good even in the face of apparent failure, and through the virtue of humility, which accepts God's mystery and trusts him even at times of darkness. (D 21)

Being persevering and patient means learning to build history together with God, because it is only by building on him and with him that the construction is firmly founded, not exploited for ideological ends but truly worthy of the human being. (HM 12-15-11)

THE FIFTH SORROWFUL MYSTERY
The Crucifixion

SELF-DENIAL

*If any man would come after me, let him deny himself
and take up his cross daily and follow me.* —Luke 9:23

Becoming men and women according to Jesus's plan
demands sacrifices, but these are by no means negative;
on the contrary, they are a help in living as people with
new hearts, in living a truly human and happy life. (I 45)

This is the demanding rule of the following of Christ: one
must be able, if necessary, to give up the whole world to
save the true values, to save the soul, to save the presence
of God in the world (Mk 8:36-37). (J 43)

Our own crosses acquire value if we consider them and
accept them as a part of the Cross of Christ, if a reflection of his light illumines them. It is by that Cross alone
that our sufferings too are ennobled and acquire their true
meaning. (J 59)

The Cross remains forever the center of the Church's life
and also of our life. In the history of the Church, there will
always be passion and persecution. And it is persecution
itself which, according to Tertullian's famous words, becomes
"the seed of Christians," the source of mission for Christians
to come. (J 138)

"All who desire to live a godly life in Christ Jesus will be
persecuted" (2 Tim 3:12), no longer by external forces, but
by the assault that the Christian must face within himself
on the part of the forces of evil. (C 88)

One aspect of becoming a Christian is having to leave behind what everyone else thinks and wants, the prevailing standards, in order to enter the light of the truth of our being, and aided by that light to find the right path. (J1 67)

The theology of glory is inseparably linked with the theology of the Cross. The Suffering Servant has the great mission to bring God's light to the world. Yet it is in the darkness of the Cross that this mission is fulfilled. (J1 85)

The closer one comes to Jesus, the more one is drawn into the mystery of his Passion. (J1 123)

All sacrifices are fulfilled in the Cross of Jesus Christ.... In him the underlying intention of all sacrifices is accomplished, namely expiation.... Jesus in this way has taken the place of the Temple ... He himself is the new Temple. (J3 38)

In his self-offering on the Cross, Jesus, as it were, brings all the sin of the world deep within the love of God and wipes it away. Accepting the Cross, entering into fellowship with Christ, means entering the realm of transformation and expiation. (J3 40)

The proclamation of the Gospel will always be marked by the sign of the Cross—this is what each generation of Jesus's disciples must learn anew. The Cross is and remains the sign of "the Son of Man": ultimately, in the battle against lies and violence, truth and love have no other weapon than the witness of suffering. (J3 49)

Again and again Jesus has to help us recognize anew that God's power is different, that the Messiah must pass through suffering into glory and must lead others along the same path. (J3 70)

It is a grace to be able to suffer for Jesus. (J3 71)

Viewed through the lens of the Last Supper and the Resurrection, we could describe the Cross as the most radical expression of God's unconditional love, as he offers himself despite all rejection on the part of men, taking men's "no" upon himself and drawing it into his "yes" (2 Cor 1:19). (J3 123)

Jesus's suffering is a Messianic Passion. It is suffering in fellowship with us and for us, in a solidarity—born of love—that already includes redemption, the victory of love. (J3 216)

Fight the inclination to avidity, pride, and impurity and practice instead the virtues of poverty and generosity, of humility and obedience, of chastity and of purity. (H 33)

It is precisely in the dark night of the Cross that divine love appears in its full grandeur; where reason no longer sees, love sees. (H 55)

"The Son of Man came to serve, and to give his life as a ransom for many" (Mk 10:45). . . . (These) are words which enshrine the meaning of Christ's mission on earth, marked by his sacrifice, by his total self-giving. (HM 10-21-12)

In every time and place, evangelization always has as its starting and finishing points Jesus Christ, the Son of God (Mk 1:1); and the Crucifix is the supremely distinctive sign of him who announces the Gospel: a sign of love and peace, a call to conversion and reconciliation . . . let us fix our gaze upon him and let us be purified by his grace. (HM 10-7-12)

Out of love (Jesus Christ) accepted the whole passion, with its anguish and its violence, even to death on the cross. In accepting it in this manner he changed it into an act of giving. This is the transformation which the world needs most, to redeem it from within, to open it to the dimensions of the Kingdom of Heaven. (HM 6-23-11)

Jesus is the Son of God who was born for us, who lived for us, who healed the sick, forgave sins and welcomed everyone. Responding to the love that comes from the Father, the Son gave his own life for us: on the cross God's merciful love reaches its highest expression. (HM 6-19-11)

In the mystery of the cross, the three divine Persons are present: the Father, who gives his Only-Begotten Son for the salvation of the world; the Son, who totally fulfills the Father's plan; the Holy Spirit—poured out by Jesus at the moment of his death—who comes to make us participants in divine life, to transform our existence so that it may be enlivened by divine love. (HM 6-19-11)

The hour of the death of Jesus, the hour of supreme love, is the hour of his highest glory. For the Church too, for every Christian, the highest glory is the Cross, which means living in charity, in total gift to God and to others. (HM 6-5-11)

Sometimes, when we speak of conversion we think solely of its demanding aspect of detachment and renunciation. Christian conversion, on the contrary, is also and above all about joy, hope and love. It is always the work of the Risen Christ, the Lord of life. (HM 6-5-11)

Faith is a gift of God but demands of us a response, a decision to follow Christ, not only when he heals and alleviates but also when he speaks of love even to the point of self-gift. (HM 12-11-11)

Without the Cross of Christ all the energy of nature remains powerless before the negative force of sin. A beneficial force greater than that which moves the cycles of nature is needed, a Good greater than that of Creation itself: a love that proceeds from the "heart" of God himself. (HM 11-3-11)

Jesus proclaims that losing oneself is the way to life. (J2 41)

The Cross is the act of the "exodus," the act of love that is accomplished to the uttermost and reaches "to the end" (Jn 13:1). And so it is the place of glory—the place of true contact and union with God, who is love (1 Jn 4:7, 16). (J2 73)

Only when faith generates the strength of renunciation and responsibility for our neighbor and for the whole of society—only then can social justice grow. (J2 77)

Following Christ is not comfortable—and Jesus never said it would be, either. (J2 109)

Job's sufferings are by anticipation sufferings in communion with Christ, who restores the honor of us all before God and shows us the way never to lose faith in God even amid the deepest darkness. (J2 162)

The failure of the Prophets is an obscure question mark hanging over the whole history of Israel, and in a certain way it constantly recurs in the history of humanity. Above all, it is also again and again the destiny of Jesus Christ: He ends up on the Cross. But that very Cross is the source of great fruitfulness. (J2 189 & 190)

The fruit the Lord expects of us is love—a love that accepts with him the mystery of the Cross, and becomes a participation in his self-giving—and hence the true justice that prepares the world for the Kingdom of God. (J2 262)

It is the language of the serpent that says to us: "Do not be afraid! Quietly eat the fruit of all the trees in the garden!" However, the true, great "Yes" to life is precisely the Cross, the true tree of life. (I 74)

It is the indispensable way for man to "lose his life," without which it is impossible for him to find it (Mk 8:31-9:1; Mt 16:21-28; Lk 9:22-27). (J2 287)

We know that through all the centuries, right up to the present, Christians—while in possession of the right confession—need the Lord to teach every generation anew that his way is not the way of earthly power and glory, but the way of the Cross. (J2 299)

Jesus's divinity belongs with the Cross—only when we put the two together do we recognize Jesus correctly...his exaltation is accomplished in no other way than in the Cross. (J2 305)

The messianic age is first and foremost the age of the Cross, and the Transfiguration—the experience of becoming light from and with the Lord—requires us to be burned by the light of the Passion and so transformed. (J2 315)

"When you have lifted up the Son of man, then you will know that I am he" (Jn 8:28). On the Cross, his Sonship, his oneness with the Father, becomes visible. The Cross is the true "height." It is the height of "love to the end" (Jn 13:1).... On the Cross, Jesus is exalted to the very "height" of the God who is love. (J2 349)

The anti-culture of death, which finds expression for example in drug use, is thus countered by an unselfish love which shows itself to be a culture of life by the very willingness to "lose itself'" (Lk 17:33) for others. (D 17)

The consciousness that, in Christ, God has given himself for us, even unto death, must inspire us to live no longer for ourselves but for him, and, with him, for others. (D 19)

It is not by sidestepping or fleeing from suffering that we are healed, but rather by our capacity for accepting it, maturing through it and finding meaning through union with Christ, who suffered with infinite love. (S 18)

Man is worth so much to God that he himself became man in order to *suffer with* man in an utterly real way—in flesh and blood—as is revealed to us in the account of Jesus's Passion. Hence in all human suffering we are joined by one who experiences and carries that suffering *with* us; hence *con-solatio* is present in all suffering, the consolation of God's compassionate love—and so the star of hope rises. (S 20)

When man and his institutions climb too high, they need to be cut back; what has become too big must be brought back to the simplicity and poverty of the Lord himself. It is only by undergoing such processes of dying away that fruitfulness endures and renews itself. (J2 260 & 261)

Unless man trusts in God, he trusts in deceit rather than in truth and thereby sinks with his life into emptiness, into death. (I 77)

At a deep level, the essence of love, the essence of genuine fruit, coincides with the idea of setting out, going towards: it means self-abandonment, self-giving, it bears within itself the sign of the cross. (HM 6-29-11)

THE GLORIOUS
MYSTERIES

THE FIRST GLORIOUS MYSTERY
The Resurrection of Jesus from the Dead

FAITH

*Blessed are those who have not seen,
and yet believe.* —John 19:27

Tradition is the communion of the faithful around their legitimate Pastors down through history, a communion that the Holy Spirit nurtures, assuring the connection between the experience of the apostolic faith, lived in the original community of the disciples, and the actual experience of Christ in his Church. (J 27)

Tradition is not the transmission of things or words, a collection of dead things. Tradition is the living river that links us to the origins, the living river in which the origins are ever present, the great river that leads us to the gates of eternity. (J 28)

The Church transmits all that she is and believes; she hands it down through worship, life, and doctrine. So it is that Tradition is the living Gospel, proclaimed by the Apostles in its integrity on the basis of the fullness of their unique and unrepeatable experience: through their activity the faith is communicated to others, even down to us, until the end of the world. (J 32)

Our faith too is always an initial one, and we have still to carry out a great journey. But it is essential that it is an open faith and that we allow ourselves to be led by Jesus, because he not only knows the Way, he *is* the Way. (J 46)

Faith must be fulfilled in life, above all, in love of neighbor and especially in dedication to the poor. It is against this background that the famous sentence must be read: "As the body apart from the spirit is dead, so faith apart from works is dead" (Jas 2:26). (J 66)

In the midst of all the temptations that exist, with all the currents of modern life, we must preserve our faith's identity. (J 103)

We must let ourselves fall, so to speak, into the communion of faith, of the Church. Believing is in itself a Catholic act. It is participation in this great certainty, which is present in the Church. (I 24)

Faith is first and foremost a personal, intimate encounter with Jesus; it is having an experience of his closeness, his friendship, and his love. It is in this way that we learn to know him even better, to love him, and to follow him more and more. May this happen to each one of us! (C 160)

Without a profound faith in God, nourished by prayer and contemplation, by an intimate relationship with the Lord, our reflections on the divine mysteries risk becoming an empty intellectual exercise and losing their credibility. (C 161)

Theology is the search for a rational understanding, as far as this is possible, of the mysteries of Christian Revelation, believed through faith . . . faith seeking understanding—to borrow a traditional, concise, and effective definition. (C 169)

Faith itself is endowed with a deep certitude based on the testimony of Scripture and on the teaching of the Church

Fathers. Faith, moreover, is reinforced by the witness of the Saints and by the inspiration of the Holy Spirit in the individual believer's soul. (c 170)

In cases of doubt and ambiguity, faith is protected and illuminated by the exercise of the Magisterium of the Church. (c 170)

These two moments—the virgin birth and the real resurrection from the tomb—are the cornerstones of faith. If God does not also have power over matter, then he simply is not God. But he does have this power, and through the conception and resurrection of Jesus Christ he has ushered in a new creation. (J1 57)

God *is* glorious, he *is* indestructible truth, eternal beauty. That is the fundamental, comforting security of our faith. (J1 76)

The word is the true, dependable reality: the solid ground on which we can stand, which holds firm even when the sun goes dark and the firmament disintegrates. The cosmic elements pass away; the word of Jesus is the true "firmament" beneath which we can stand and remain. (J3 51)

Jesus's Incarnation is ordered toward his offering of himself for men, and this in turn is ordered toward the Resurrection: were it otherwise, Christianity would not be true. (J3 105)

The Christian faith stands or falls with the truth of the testimony that Christ is risen from the dead....Only if Jesus is risen has anything really new occurred that changes the world and the situation of mankind. Then he becomes the criterion on which we can rely. For then God has truly revealed himself. (J3 241 & 242)

The power that imposes a limit on evil is Divine Mercy.... God's own power—by Divine Mercy. The Lamb is stronger than the dragon, we could say together with the Book of Revelation. (I 55)

He is truly risen. He is alive. Let us entrust ourselves to him, knowing that we are on the right path. With Thomas let us place our hands into Jesus's pierced side and confess: "My Lord and my God!" (Jn 20:28). (J3 277)

You too offer to the Lord the gold of your lives, namely, your freedom to follow him out of love, responding faithfully to his call....Walk together in unity. Always be faithful to Christ and to the Church. (G 23 & 65)

Faith is not merely a dogmatism complete in itself that puts an end to seeking, that extinguishes man's great thirst, but it directs the great pilgrimage towards the infinite; we, as believers, are always simultaneously seekers and finders. (G 95)

Thomas Aquinas showed that a natural harmony exists between Christian faith and reason. And this was the great achievement of Thomas, who, at that time of clashes between two cultures—that time when it seemed that faith would have to give in to reason—showed that they go hand in hand. (H 67)

Faith consolidates, integrates, and illumines the heritage of truth that human reason acquires ... both stem from the one source of all truth, the divine *Logos*, which is active in both contexts, that of creation and that of redemption. (H 73)

The entire history of theology is basically the exercise of this task of the mind, which shows the intelligibility of faith, its articulation and inner harmony, its reasonableness and its ability to further human good. (H 74)

All Christians can attain the lofty perspectives of the "Sermon on the Mount" if they live an authentic relationship of faith in Christ, if they are open to the action of his Holy Spirit. (H 76)

It is reasonable to believe in God, who reveals himself, and in the testimony of the Apostles: they were few, simple, and poor, grief-stricken by the Crucifixion of their Teacher. Yet many wise, noble, and rich people converted very soon after hearing their preaching. (H 84)

Faith is the light that guides every decision. (H 183)

In order to proclaim the Gospel and to enable all who do not yet know Jesus, or who have abandoned him, to cross the threshold of the door of faith once again and to live communion with God, it is indispensable to know in depth the meaning of the truths contained in the Profession of Faith. (HM 12-31-12)

Live once again the mystery of this faithfulness of God, on which you are called to found your lives, as on a firm rock. In celebrating and living this itinerary of faith with the whole Church, you will experience that Jesus Christ is the one Lord of the cosmos and of history, without whom every human project risks coming to nothing. (HM 12-1-12)

Jesus sends his Church not to a single group, but to the whole human race, and thus he unites it, in faith, in one people, in order to save it. (HM 11-24-12)

Jesus is the center of the Christian faith. The Christian believes in God whose face was revealed by Jesus Christ. He is the fulfillment of the Scriptures and their definitive interpreter. Jesus Christ is not only the object of the faith but, as it says in the *Letter to the Hebrews,* he is "the pioneer and the perfecter of our faith" (Hb 12:2). (HM 10-11-12)

The eternal presence of God resounds in the faith, transcending time, yet it can only be welcomed by us in our own unrepeatable today. Therefore I believe that the most important thing . . . is to revive in the whole Church that positive tension, that yearning to announce Christ again to contemporary man. (HM 10-11-12)

In faith we open the doors of our existence so that God may enter us, so that God can be the power that gives life and a path to our existence. (HM 8-15-12)

In the sacraments the Lord touches us through the elements of creation. The unity between creation and redemption is made visible. The sacraments are an expression of the physicality of our faith, which embraces the whole person, body and soul. (HM 4-21-11)

Is it perhaps the case that the West, the heartlands of Christianity, are tired of their faith, bored by their history and culture, and no longer wish to know faith in Jesus Christ? We have reason to cry out at this time to God: "Do not allow us to become a 'non-people'! Make us recognize you again!" (HM 4-21-11)

Christ's disciples are called to reawaken in themselves and in others the longing for God and the joy of living in him and bearing witness to him, on the basis of what is always a deeply personal question: why do I believe? (HM 12-31-11)

We must give primacy to truth, seeing the combination of faith and reason as two wings with which the human spirit can rise to the contemplation of the Truth. (HM 12-31-11)

It is my duty to recommend you to be alert and to deepen your knowledge of the reasons for faith and for the Christian message; so that you may transmit it in a way that guarantees the authentic millenary tradition of the Church. (HM 12-11-11)

Let us allow Christ to free us from the world of the past! Our faith in him, which frees us from all our fear and miseries, gives us access to a new world, a world where justice and truth are not a byword, a world of interior freedom and of peace with ourselves, with our neighbors and with God. (HM 11-20-11)

How is my personal relationship with God: in prayer, in participation at Sunday Mass, in exploring my faith through meditation on Sacred Scripture and study of the Catechism of the Catholic Church?...The renewal of the Church will only come about through openness to conversion and through renewed faith. (HM 9-25-11)

Faith always includes as an essential element the fact that it is shared with others. No one can believe alone. We receive the faith—as Saint Paul tells us—through hearing, and hearing is part of being together, in spirit and in body. (HM 9-24-11)

Peter responds with what is the first confession of faith: "You are the Messiah, the Son of the living God." Faith is more than just empirical or historical facts; it is an ability to grasp the mystery of Christ's person in all its depth.... Faith is not the result of human effort, of human reasoning, but rather a gift of God. (HM 8-21-11)

Faith does not simply provide information about who Christ is; rather, it entails a personal relationship with Christ, a surrender of our whole person, with all our understanding, will and feelings, to God's self-revelation. (HM 8-21-11)

The people who are persecuted for righteousness' sake are those who live by God's righteousness—by faith. Because man constantly strives for emancipation from God's will in order to follow himself alone, faith will always appear as a contradiction to the "world"—to the ruling powers at any given time. (J2 89)

There must always be people in the Church who leave everything in order to follow the Lord, people who depend radically on God, on his bounty by which we are fed—people, then, who in this way present a sign of faith that shakes us out of our heedlessness and the weakness of our faith. (J2 152)

God does not fail; we may be unfaithful, but he is always faithful (2 Tim 2:13). He finds new and greater ways for his love. (J2 258)

The highest things, the things that really matter, we cannot achieve on our own; we have to accept them as gifts and enter into the dynamic of the gift.... This happens in the context of faith in Jesus, who is dialogue—a living relationship with the Father—and who wants to become Word and love in us as well. (J2 268)

We have come to believe in God's love: in these words the Christian can express the fundamental decision of his life. Being Christian is not the result of an ethical choice or a lofty idea, but the encounter with an event, a person, which gives life a new horizon and a decisive direction. (D 1)

Every culture has burdens from which it must be freed and shadows from which it must emerge. The Christian faith, by becoming incarnate in cultures and at the same time transcending them, can help them grow in universal brotherhood and solidarity. (CV 33)

THE SECOND GLORIOUS MYSTERY
The Ascension of Jesus into Heaven

HOPE

Ask, and it will be given you; seek, and you will find;
knock, and the door shall be opened to you. —Luke 11:9

When faith meets with dark nights, in which the presence of God is no longer "felt" or "seen," friendship with Jesus guarantees that in reality nothing can ever separate us from his love. (I 28)

We know that Jesus adapts himself to this weakness of ours. We follow him with our poor capacity to love, and we know that Jesus is good and he accepts us. . . . Jesus does not exclude anyone from his friendship. (J 48 & 82)

Only the sacrificed Lamb can open the sealed scroll and reveal its content, and give meaning to this history that so often seems senseless. He alone can draw from it instructions and teachings for the life of Christians, to whom his victory over death brings the message and guarantee of victory that they too will undoubtedly obtain. (J 78 & 79)

(Our Lord) made the important statement. "Those who are well have no need of a physician, but those who are sick; I came not to call the righteous, but sinners" (Mk 2:17). The good news of the Gospel consists precisely in this offering: God's grace to the sinner! (J 83)

The Spirit is a generous down payment given to us by God himself as a deposit and, at the same time, a guarantee of our future inheritance (2 Cor 1:22; Eph 1:13-14). (J 123)

Only if there is God, this great hope to which I aspire, can I take the small steps of my life and thus learn charity. (C 72)

We see on one side the beauty of Creation and, on the other, the destruction wrought by the fault of man. But we see in the Son of God, who descends to renew nature, the sea of love that God has for man. (C 104)

The fundamental word that serves to designate the entire Christian message: *Gospel—good news.* (J1 27)

The personal character of righteousness (is) the trust in God that gives man hope. (J1 40)

The Creator is also our Redeemer. Hence the conception and birth of Jesus from the Virgin Mary is a fundamental element of our faith and a radiant sign of hope. (J1 57)

In the new birth of the resurrection, Jesus is no longer merely the first in dignity, he now ushers in a new humanity. Once he has broken through the iron door of death, there are many more who can pass through with him — many who in baptism have died with him and risen with him. (J1 70)

Jesus does not come as a destroyer. He does not come bearing the sword of the revolutionary. He comes with the gift of healing. . . . He reveals God as the one who loves and his power as the power of love. (J3 23)

His Cross and His exaltation is the Day of Atonement for the world, in which the whole of world history — in the face of all human sin and its destructive consequences — finds its meaning and is aligned with its true purpose and destiny. (J3 79)

The Christian will remember that Jesus's blood speaks a different language from the blood of Abel (Heb 12:24): it does not cry out for vengeance and punishment; it brings reconciliation. It is not poured out *against* anyone; it is poured out *for* many, for all. (J3 187)

The pathway to God is open. (J3 209)

In the history of Christian devotion, the good thief has become an image of hope — an image of the consoling certainty that God's mercy can reach us even in our final moments, that even after a misspent life, the plea for his gracious favor is not made in vain. (J3 212)

We can always call on him; we can always be certain that he sees and hears us. (J3 284)

Faith in Christ's return is the second pillar of the Christian confession. He who took flesh and now retains his humanity forever, he who has eternally opened up within God a space for humanity, now calls the whole world into this open space in God, so that in the end God may be all in all and the Son may hand over to the Father the whole world that is gathered together in him (Cor 15:20-28). Herein is contained the certainty of hope. (J3 287)

"Surely I am coming soon. Amen. Come, Lord Jesus!" (Rev 22:20). It is the prayer of one who loves, one who is surrounded in the besieged city by all the dangers and terrors of destruction and can only wait for the arrival of the beloved who has the power to end the siege and to bring salvation. It is the hope-filled cry for Jesus to draw near. (J3 288 & 289)

Can we pray for the coming of Jesus? Can we sincerely say: *"Marana tha!* Come, Lord Jesus!"* Yes, we can. And not only that: we must! We pray for anticipations of his world-changing presence. (J3 292)

The merciful goodness of God always allows us to make a fresh start in our lives. (G 12)

Be completely convinced of this: Christ takes from you nothing that is beautiful and great, but brings everything to perfection for the glory of God, the happiness of men and women, and the salvation of the world. (G 39)

Christ's works do not go backward, they do not fail but progress. (H 45)

God's passionate love for his people — for humanity — is at the same time a forgiving love. It is so great that it turns God against himself, his love against his justice. Here Christians can see a dim prefiguration of the mystery of the Cross. (I 46)

Christian faith is strengthened in considering the mystery of the Incarnation; hope is strengthened at the thought that the Son of God came among us, as one of us, to communicate his own divinity to men; charity is revived because there is no more obvious sign of God's love for us than the sight of the Creator of the universe making himself a creature, one of us. (H 84)

In the mysterious designs of Providence, God can draw a greater good even from evil. (H 163 & 164)

God's promises are ever greater than our expectations. If we present to God, to his immense love, the purest and deepest desires of our heart, we shall never be disappointed. (H 164)

The human being of every age searches for a glimmer of light that brings hope, that still speaks of life. . . .We respond with faith in God, with a gaze of firm hope founded on the death and Resurrection of Jesus Christ. (HM 11-3-12)

Living faith opens the heart to the grace of God which frees us from pessimism. Today, more than ever, evangelizing means witnessing to the new life, transformed by God, and thus showing the path. (HM 10-11-12)

With God, even in difficult times or moments of crisis, there is always a horizon of hope: the Incarnation tells us that we are never alone, that God has come to humanity and that he accompanies us. (HM 10-4-12)

Not only are we restless for God: God's heart is restless for us. God is waiting for us. He is looking for us. He knows no rest either, until he finds us. God's heart is restless, and that is why he set out on the path towards us—to Bethlehem, to Calvary. (HM 1-6-12)

We need both sun and rain, festivity and adversity, times of purification and testing, as well as times of joyful journeying with the Gospel. In hindsight we can thank God for both: for the challenges and the joys, for the dark times and the glad times. In both, we can recognize the constant presence of his love, which unfailingly supports and sustains us. (HM 6-29-11)

Our faith and our hope are addressed to God (1 Pt 1:21): they are addressed to God because they are rooted in him, founded on his love and on his fidelity. (HM 5-8-11)

Creation itself remains good, life remains good, because at the beginning is good Reason, God's creative love. Hence the world can be saved. Hence we can and must place ourselves on the side of reason, freedom and love—on the side of God. (HM 4-23-11)

God loves us so much that he suffered for us, that from his death there might emerge a new, definitive and healed life. (HM 4-23-11)

There is no more room for anxiety in the face of time that passes, never to return; now there is room for unlimited trust in God, by whom we know we are loved, for whom we live and to whom our life is directed as we await his definitive return. (HM 12-31-11)

Our existence is no longer left to the impersonal forces of natural and historical processes, our house can be built on the rock: we can plan our history, the history of humanity, not in Utopia but in the certainty that the God of Jesus Christ is present and goes with us. (HM 12-15-11)

Even in the midst of so many doubts and difficulties, joy exists because God exists and is with us! (HM 12-11-11)

God desires the salvation of his people. He desires our salvation, my salvation, the salvation of every single person. He is always close to us, especially in times of danger and radical change, and his heart aches for us, he reaches out to us. We need to open ourselves to him so that the power of his mercy can touch our hearts. (HM 9-25-11)

Where God is, there is a future. (HM 9-24-11)

The sign of God is overflowing generosity. We see it in the multiplication of the loaves; we see it again and again—most of all, though, at the center of salvation history, in the fact that he lavishly spends himself for the lowly creature, man. This abundant giving is his "glory." (J2 252)

The Cross is not an end, but a new beginning. (J2 258)

According to Christian faith, "redemption"—salvation—is not simply a given. Redemption is offered to us in the sense that we have been given hope, trustworthy hope, by virtue of which we can face our present: the present, even if it is arduous, can be lived and accepted if it leads towards a goal, if we can be sure of this goal, and if this goal is great enough to justify the effort of the journey. (S 1)

Anyone who does not know God, even though he may enter-
tain all kinds of hopes, is ultimately without hope, without
the great hope that sustains the whole of life (Eph 2:12). Man's
great, true hope which holds firm in spite of all disappoint-
ments can only be God—God who has loved us and who
continues to love us "to the end," until all "is accomplished"
(Jn 13:1 and 19:30). (S 14)

A world without God is a world without hope (Eph 2:12).
Only God can create justice. And faith gives us the certainty
that he does so. The image of the Last Judgement is not
primarily an image of terror, but an image of hope; for us
it may even be the decisive image of hope. (S 20)

Man is not a lost atom in a random universe: he is God's
creature, whom God chose to endow with an immortal soul
and whom he has always loved. (CV 15)

Hope encourages reason and gives it the strength to direct
the will. It is already present in faith, indeed it is called
forth by faith. Charity in truth feeds on hope and, at the
same time, manifests it. (CV 18)

In the figure of Matthew, the Gospels present to us a true
and proper paradox: those who seem to be the farthest
from holiness can even become a model of the acceptance
of God's mercy and offer a glimpse of its marvelous effects
in their own lives. (J 83)

The fruitfulness of the Christian faith and tradition we
must rekindle, because it has within it new strength for the
future. (G 30)

We must not yield to fear or pessimism. Rather, we must
cultivate optimism and hope. (G 77)

God makes himself a man like us to give us a hope that is
sure: if we follow him, if we are consistent in living our

Christian life, he will draw us to him, he will lead us to communion with him; and there will be in our hearts true joy and true peace, even in difficulty, even in moments of weakness. (HM 12-16-12)

In our own day, too, the boat of the Church travels against the headwind of history through the turbulent ocean of time. Often it looks as if it is bound to sink. But the Lord is there, and he comes at the right moment. "I go away, and I will come back to you"—that is the essence of Christian trust, the reason for our joy. (J3 285)

Whoever believes in Christ has a future. For God has no desire for what is withered, dead, and finally discarded: he wants what is fruitful and alive, he wants life in its fullness and he gives us life in its fullness. (HM 9-22-11)

THE THIRD GLORIOUS MYSTERY
The Descent of the Holy Spirit

LOVE OF GOD

You shall love the Lord your God with all your heart, and with all your soul, and with all your mind, and with all your strength. —Mark 12:30

The essential constituent of God is love ... all God's activity is born from love and impressed with love: all that God does, he does out of love and with love, even if we are not always immediately able to understand that this is love, true love. (J 73)

Saint Augustine (said): "If you see charity, you see the Trinity".... The Spirit immerses us in the very rhythm of divine life, which is a life of love, enabling us to share personally in relations between the Father and the Son. (J 122)

In the end love sees more than reason. Where the light of love shines, the shadows of reason are dispelled; love sees; love is an eye, and experience gives us more than reflection. (C 29)

Charity is the greatest of the virtues. (C 35)

With merely theological research God cannot truly be known as he is. Love alone reaches him. (C 92)

God's love develops in us if we stay united to him with prayer and with listening to his word, with an open heart. Divine love alone prompts us to open our hearts to others. (C 144)

For every disciple of Jesus the essential thing is to grow in love; thus we grow in the knowledge of Christ himself, so as to be able to say with Saint Paul: "It is no longer I who live, but Christ who lives in me" (Gal 2:20). (c 145)

Knowledge only grows if one loves truth. Love becomes intelligence and authentic theology wisdom of the heart, which directs and sustains the faith and life of believers. (c 168)

This radical vocation to love for God is the secret of a successful and happy life. (c 194)

Our hearts are made of flesh and blood, and when we love God, who is Love itself, how can we fail to express in this relationship with the Lord our most human feelings, such as tenderness, sensitivity, and delicacy? In becoming man, the Lord himself wanted to love us with a heart of flesh! (c 194)

Is it not perhaps true that we only truly know *who* and *what* we love? Without a certain fondness, one knows no one and nothing! And this applies first of all to the knowledge of God and his mysteries, which exceed our mental capacity to understand: God is known if he is loved! (c 195)

(Let us) make the basic decision in our lives which gives meaning and value to all our other decisions: to love God and, through love of him, to love our neighbor; only in this manner shall we be able to find true joy, an anticipation of eternal beatitude. (c 196)

Together with a young Saint, a Doctor of the Church, Thérèse of the Child Jesus, let us tell the Lord that we, too, want to live on love. (c 196)

It remains true that we could not love if we were not first loved by God. God's grace always precedes us, embraces us and carries us. But it also remains true that man is called to love in return, he does not remain an unwilling tool of God's omnipotence: he can love in return or he can refuse God's love. (j1 76)

Christ, at the Father's right hand, is not far away from us. At most we are far from him, but the path that joins us to one another is open. And this path is not a matter of space travel of a cosmic-geographical nature: it is the "space travel" of the heart, from the dimension of self-enclosed isolation to the new dimension of world-embracing divine love. (J3 286)

Love knows no "why"; it is a free gift to which one responds with the gift of self. (G 46)

The better you know Jesus, the more his mystery attracts you. The more you discover him, the more you are moved to seek him. This is a movement of the Spirit which lasts throughout life. (G 47)

The *Poverello* of Assisi, notwithstanding the intellectual debates of his time, had shown with his whole life the primacy of love. He was a living icon of Christ in love with Christ, and thus he made the figure of the Lord present in his time—he convinced his contemporaries, not with his words, but rather with his life. (H 53)

Love goes beyond reason, it sees farther, it enters more profoundly into God's mystery. (H 55)

Love transcends knowledge and is capable of perceiving ever better than thought, but it is always the love of God who is "Logos." (H 92)

In our life the essential thing is to believe that God is close to us and loves us in Jesus Christ and, therefore, to cultivate a deep love for him and for his Church. We on earth are witnesses of this love. (H 93)

Man is created in the image of God and is therefore called to build with God a wonderful history of love, allowing himself to be totally involved in his initiative. (H 144)

Every believer feels the need to be conformed to the sentiments of the heart of Christ in order to love God and his neighbor as Christ himself loves. (H 156)

We can all let our hearts be transformed and learn to love like Christ in a familiarity with him that is nourished by prayer, by meditation on the word of God, and by the sacraments, above all by receiving Holy Communion frequently and with devotion. (H 156)

Love embraces the whole of the reality of God and of the human being, of Heaven and of earth, of the Church and of the world. (H 182)

The true content of the Law, its *summa*, is love for God and for one's neighbor. But this twofold love is not simply saccharine. It bears within itself the precious cargo of patience, humility, and growth in the conforming of our will to God's will, to the will of Jesus Christ, our friend. (HM 6-29-11)

Eucharistic communion requires faith, but faith requires love; otherwise, even with faith, it is dead. (HM 4-21-11)

That restlessness for God, that journeying towards him, so as to know and love him better, must not be extinguished in us. In this sense we should always remain catechumens. (HM 4-21-11)

The whole of the Divine Law can be summed up in love. (HM 10-23-11)

We are all invited to be the Lord's guests, to enter his banquet with faith, but we must put on and take care of the wedding garment: charity, to live in the profound love of God and neighbor. (HM 10-9-11)

It is only on the way of love, whose paths are described in the Sermon on the Mount, that the richness of life and the greatness of man's calling are opened up. (J2 99)

This orientation pervasively shaping our whole conscious-ness, this silent presence of God at the heart of our thinking, our meditating, and our being, is what we mean by "prayer without ceasing." This is ultimately what we mean by love of God, which is at the same time the condition and the driving force behind love of neighbor. (J2 130)

The path of love . . . is at the same time a path of conversion. If man is to petition God in the right way, he must stand in the truth. And the truth is: first God, first his Kingdom (Mt 6:33). The first thing we must do is step outside ourselves and open ourselves to God. Nothing can turn out right if our relation to God is not rightly ordered. (J2 134)

Whoever truly wishes to heal man must see him in his wholeness and must know that his ultimate healing can only be God's love. (J2 177)

Man lives on truth and on being loved: on being loved by the truth. He needs God, the God who draws close to him, interprets for him the meaning of life, and thus points him toward the path of life. (J2 279)

Love looks to the eternal. Love is indeed "ecstasy," not in the sense of a moment of intoxication, but rather as a jour-ney, an ongoing exodus out of the closed inward-looking self towards its liberation through self-giving, and thus towards authentic self-discovery and indeed the discovery of God. (D 4)

Anyone who wishes to give love must also receive love as a gift. Certainly, as the Lord tells us, one can become a source from which rivers of living water flow (Jn 7:37-38). Yet to become such a source, one must constantly drink anew from the original source, which is Jesus Christ, from whose pierced heart flows the love of God (Jn 19:34). (D 5)

God loves man ... So great is God's love for man that by becoming man he follows him even into death, and so reconciles justice and love. (D 6)

Love grows through love. Love is "divine" because it comes from God and unites us to God; through this unifying process it makes us a "we" which transcends our divisions and makes us one. (D 10)

It is not science that redeems man: man is redeemed by love. This applies even in terms of this present world. (s 13)

Man was created for greatness—for God himself; he was created to be filled by God. But his heart is too small for the greatness to which it is destined. It must be stretched. (s 16)

The search for love and truth is purified and liberated by Jesus Christ from the impoverishment that our humanity brings to it, and he reveals to us in all its fullness the initiative of love and the plan for true life that God has prepared for us. In Christ, *charity in truth* becomes the Face of his Person. (CV 1)

Charity is love received and given. It is "grace" (*charis*). Its source is the wellspring of the Father's love for the Son, in the Holy Spirit. Love comes down to us from the Son. It is creative love, through which we have our being; it is redemptive love, through which we are recreated. Love is revealed and made present by Christ (Jn 13:1). (CV 2)

Charity overcomes all resistance, and whoever loves joyfully performs every sacrifice. . . . Let us learn from Saint Catherine to love Christ and the Church with courage, intensely and sincerely. (H 105 & 158)

It is beautiful to live because I am loved and it is the Truth who loves me. (HM 6-12-11)

God saves. (J1 30)

THE FOURTH GLORIOUS MYSTERY
The Assumption of Mary into Heaven

DESIRE FOR HEAVEN

*Come, O blessed of my Father, inherit the
kingdom prepared for you from the foundation
of the world.* —Matthew 25:34

It is true that on our journey toward God we are still very far from him.... In the end the journey to God is God himself, who makes himself close to us in Jesus Christ. (C 29)

(Jesus) returns home, and he leads others home. He is always on the path toward God and thus he leads the way back from exile to the homeland, back to all that is authentic and true. Jesus, the true Son, himself went into "exile" in a very deep sense, in order to lead all of us home from exile. (J1 111 & 112)

"Eternal life" is life itself, real life, which can also be lived in the present age and is no longer challenged by physical death. This is the point: to seize "life" here and now, real life that can no longer be destroyed by anything or anyone. (J3 83)

Man has found life when he adheres to him who is himself Life.... Death may remove him from the biosphere, but the life that reaches beyond it—real life—remains. This life, which John calls *zoe* as opposed to *bios,* is man's goal. (J3 85)

If there really is a God, is he not able to create a new dimension of human existence, a new dimension of reality altogether? Is not creation actually waiting for this last and highest "evolutionary leap," for the union of the finite with the infinite, for the union of man and God, for the conquest of death? (J3 247)

The more deeply we penetrate the splendor of divine love, the greater will be our discoveries and the more beautiful it will be to travel on and to know that our seeking has no end and, hence, finding has no end, and therefore eternity is at the same time the joy of seeking and finding. (G 95 & 96)

The true is also the good, and the good is also the true; to see God is to love, and to love is to see. (H 53)

However lofty and pure it may be, all we manage to think and say about the faith is infinitely exceeded by God's greatness and beauty, which will be fully revealed to us in Heaven. (H 69)

May Mary Most Holy help us to receive this infinite love of God which we will enjoy eternally to the full in Heaven, when our soul is at last united to God forever in the Communion of Saints. (H 93)

One day we shall be immersed in divine love, in the joy of eternity with God. (H 134)

Meditation on our eternal destiny, on our call to participate forever in the beatitude of God as well as on the tragic possibility of damnation, contributes to living with serenity and dedication and to facing the reality of death, ever preserving full trust in God's goodness. (H 230)

We often come across indifference to God. However, I think that in the inner depths of all those who live far from God — also among your peers — there is an inner longing for the infinite, for transcendence. (HM 12-1-12)

Faith tells us that the true immortality for which we hope is not an idea, a concept, but a relationship of full communion with the living God: it is resting in his hands, in his love, and becoming in him one with all the brothers and sisters that he has created and redeemed, with all Creation. (HM 11-3-12)

Our hope lies in the love of God that shines resplendent from the Cross of Christ who lets Jesus's words to the good thief, "Today you will be with me in Paradise" (Lk 23:43), resound in our heart. This is life in its fullness: life in God; a life of which we now have only a glimpse as one sees blue sky through fog. (HM 11-3-12)

Our justice is based on faith in Christ. He is the "just man," foretold in all the Scriptures; it is thanks to his Pascal Mystery that, by crossing the threshold of death, our eyes will behold God, contemplate his face (Job 19:27). (HM 11-3-12)

We are pilgrims . . . we must always be on the way to another dwelling, towards our final home, the Eternal City, the dwelling place of God and the people he has redeemed (Rev 21:3). (HM 10-4-12)

God expects us, waits for us, we do not go out into a void, we are expected. God is expecting us and, on going to that other world, we find the goodness of the Mother, we find our loved ones, we find eternal Love. God is waiting for us: this is our great joy. (HM 8-15-12)

We know that God prepares for all men and women new heavens and a new earth, in which peace and justice reign— and in faith we perceive the new world which is our true homeland. (HM 6-23-11)

Together with Jesus, we are setting out on pilgrimage along the high road that leads to the living God. This is the ascent that matters. This is the journey which Jesus invites us to make. (HM 4-17-11)

"Come, O blessed of my Father, inherit the kingdom prepared for you from the foundation of the world" (Mt 25:34). Let us receive this word of blessing which the Son of Man will, on the Day of Judgement, address to those who have recognized his presence in the lowliest of their brethren, with a heart free and full of the love of the Lord! (HM 11-20-11)

At the origin of hope is the desire of the Father and the Son, which we heard about in the Gospel....."Father, I desire that those whom you have given me, may be with me where I am" (Jn 17:24). (HM 11-3-11)

In Christ, we have the promise of definitive redemption and the certain hope of future blessings. Through Christ we know that we are not walking towards the abyss, the silence of nothingness or death, but are rather pilgrims on the way to a promised land, on the way to him who is our end and our beginning. (HM 8-21-11)

Jesus has to enter into the drama of human existence, for that belongs to the core of his mission; he has to penetrate it completely, down to its uttermost depths, in order to find the "lost sheep," to bear it on his shoulders, and to bring it home. (J2 26)

Read in the light of Jesus's great discourse on the bread of life, the miracle of the manna naturally points beyond itself to the new world in which the Logos — the eternal Word of God — will be our bread, the food of the eternal wedding banquet. (J2 155)

This is Jesus's great promise: to give life in abundance. Everyone wants life in abundance.... Jesus promises that he will show the sheep where to find "pasture" — something they can live on — and that he will truly lead them to the springs of life. (J2 278)

Jesus's garment of white light at the Transfiguration speaks of our future as well. In apocalyptic literature, white garments

are an expression of heavenly beings—the garments of
angels and of the elect. (J2 310)

In the end, man both needs and longs for just one thing: life,
the fullness of life—"happiness." In one passage in John's
Gospel, Jesus calls this one simple thing for which we long
"perfect joy" (Jn 16:24). (J2 353)

We see as a distinguishing mark of Christians the fact that
they have a future: it is not that they know the details of
what awaits them, but they know in general terms that
their life will not end in emptiness. Only when the future
is certain as a positive reality does it become possible to
live the present as well. (S 1 & 2)

When the Letter to the Hebrews says that Christians here
on earth do not have a permanent homeland, but seek one
which lies in the future (Heb 11:13-16; Phil 3:20), this does
not mean for one moment that they live only for the future:
present society is recognized by Christians as an exile; they
belong to a new society which is the goal of their common
pilgrimage. (S 3)

Jesus expresses it in Saint John's Gospel: "I will see you
again and your hearts will rejoice, and no one will take your
joy from you" (Jn 16:22). We must think along these lines
if we want to understand the object of Christian hope, to
understand what it is that our faith, our being with Christ,
leads us to expect. (S 8)

Man has need of a hope that goes further. It becomes clear
that only something infinite will suffice for him, something
that will always be more than he can ever attain. (S 15)

We cannot—to use the classical expression—"merit" Heaven
through our works. Heaven is always more than we could

merit, just as being loved is never something "merited," but always a gift.... Heaven far exceeds what we can merit. (s 18)

Yes, there is a resurrection of the flesh. There is justice. There is an "undoing" of past suffering, a reparation that sets things aright. For this reason, faith in the Last Judgement is first and foremost hope—the need for which was made abundantly clear in the upheavals of recent centuries. (s 20)

The purely individual need for a fulfillment that is denied to us in this life, for an everlasting love that we await, is certainly an important motive for believing that man was made for eternity. (s 20)

Every man and woman, through baptism in the death and Resurrection of Christ, participates in the victory of the One who defeated death first, setting out on a journey of transformation that is manifested from this moment in a newness of life that will reach its fullness at the end of time. (HM 1-25-12)

Man must face the daily challenge of vice that distances him on the way toward God and of virtue that benefits him. The invitation is to distance oneself from evil in order to glorify God and, after a virtuous existence, enter the life that consists "wholly of joy." (H 99)

Hope alone renders us capable of living charity; hope in which we transcend the things of every day; we do not expect success in our earthly days, but we look forward to the revelation of God himself at last. (c 72)

Believing means entrusting one's life to the One who alone can give it fullness in time and open it to a hope beyond time. (HM 12-1-12)

"God is love, and he who abides in love abides in God, and

God abides in him" (1 Jn 4:16). These words from the First Letter of John express with remarkable clarity the heart of the Christian faith: the Christian image of God and the resulting image of mankind and its destiny. (HM 1-13-13)

Man can indeed enter into union with God.... But this union is no mere fusion, a sinking in the nameless ocean of the Divine; it is a unity which creates love, a unity in which both God and man remain themselves and yet become fully one. As Saint Paul says: "He who is united to the Lord becomes one spirit with him" (1 Cor 6:17). (D 7)

The resurrection of Jesus strengthens our hope of true consolation. (J1 113)

The life of the soul is a continuous celebration of the Holy Spirit which gives us a glimpse of the glory of union with God in eternity. (H 202)

THE FIFTH GLORIOUS MYSTERY
The Crowning of Mary
Queen of Heaven and Earth

DEVOTION TO MARY

Behold, your mother! —John 19:27

After Mary, a pure reflection of the light of Christ, it is from the Apostles, through their word and witness, that we receive the truth of Christ.... Discover the true face of the Church in Mary, in the Saints. (J 7 & 8 & C 92)

Having become a disciple of her Son, Mary manifested total trust in him at Cana (Jn 2:5) and followed him to the foot of the Cross, where she received from him a maternal mission for all his disciples of all times, represented by John (Jn 19:25-27). (J 151)

Mary (is) a model of the Church, a model for all of us, because Christ must also be born in and among us. (C 91)

Only God is truly his "father." The human genealogy has a certain significance in terms of world history. And yet in the end it is Mary, the lowly virgin from Nazareth, in whom a new beginning takes place, in whom human existence starts afresh. (J1 8)

Through Mary we are led to Jesus. (C 160)

Mary's greatness consists in the fact that she wants to magnify God, not herself. (I 53)

Mary appears as a fearless woman.... At the same time she stands before us as a woman of great interiority, who holds heart and mind in harmony and seeks to understand the context, the overall significance of God's message. In this way, she becomes an image of the Church. (J1 33)

From (Mary's) lips, from her heart, the answer comes: "Let it be to me according to your word." It is the moment of free, humble yet magnanimous obedience in which the loftiest choice of human freedom is made. (J1 36)

Mary becomes a mother through her "yes." The Church Fathers sometimes expressed this by saying that Mary conceived through her ear—that is to say: through her hearing. Through her obedience, the Word entered into her and became fruitful in her. (J1 36 & 37)

The contradiction against the Son is also directed against the mother and it cuts her to the heart. For her, the Cross of radical contradiction becomes the sword that pierces through her soul. From Mary we can learn what true compassion is: quite unsentimentally assuming the sufferings of others as one's own. (J1 86 & 87)

The presence of Our Lady ... introduces everyone to an encounter with Christ in the silence of meditation, prayer and fraternity. Mary helps us to meet the Lord above all in the celebration of the Eucharist, when, in the Word and in the consecrated Bread, he becomes our daily spiritual nourishment. (G 48)

The Immaculate Heart of Mary ... watches over each one of you with a mother's love. Have recourse to Mary, often and with confidence. (G 49)

Because of the Incarnation, in no creature as in (Mary) do the three Divine Persons dwell and feel delight and joy at dwelling in her soul full of grace. Through her intercession we may obtain every help. (H 85)

The Immaculate Conception is the masterpiece of the redemption brought about by Christ because the very power of his love and his mediation obtained that the Mother be preserved from original sin. Therefore Mary is totally redeemed by Christ, but already before her conception. (H 90)

Praise the Son with the heart of the Mother . . . praise Mary with the heart of the Son. (H 113 & 114)

In the great Christian tradition, the woman is accorded special dignity and — always based on the example of Mary, Queen of Apostles — a place of her own in the Church, which, without coinciding with the ordained priesthood, is equally important for the spiritual growth of the Community. (H 139)

Devotion to Mary will be of great comfort to us at the moment of our death. (H 230)

The singular human existence of the Son of God is accompanied by his Most Holy Mother, who, alone among all creatures, we venerate as Immaculate and full of grace. (HM 11-3-12)

The greatest event in our history (is) the Incarnation; the Word became flesh and Mary, the handmaid of the Lord, is the privileged channel through which God came to dwell among us (Jn 1:14). Mary offered her very body; she placed her entire being at the disposal of God's will. (HM 10-4-12)

The will of Mary coincides with the will of the Son in the Father's unique project of love and, in her, heaven and earth are united, God the Creator is united to his creature. God becomes man, and Mary becomes a "living house" for the Lord, a temple where the Most High dwells. (HM 10-4-12)

Mary, who is the Mother of Christ, is also our mother, and she opens to us the door to her home, she helps us enter into the will of her Son. So it is faith which gives us a home in this world, which brings us together in one family and which makes all of us brothers and sisters. (HM 10-4-12)

Mother of the "yes," you who heard Jesus, speak to us of him; tell us of your journey, that we may follow him on the path of faith; help us to proclaim him, that each person may welcome him and become the dwelling place of God. Amen! (HM 10-4-12)

Mary herself prophetically pronounces a few words that orientate us in this perspective. She says: "For behold, henceforth all generations will call me blessed" (Lk 1:48). It is a prophecy for the whole history of the Church. These words of the Magnificat, recorded by St. Luke, indicate that praising the Blessed Virgin, Mother of God, intimately united to Christ her Son, regards the Church of all ages and of all places. (HM 8-15-12)

Why is Mary glorified by her Assumption into Heaven? St. Luke sees the roots of the exaltation and praise of Mary in Elizabeth's words: "Blessed is she who believed" (Lk 1:56). And the Magnificat, this canticle to God, alive and active in history is a hymn of faith and love, which springs from the heart of the Virgin. (HM 8-15-12)

Mary expecting the birth of her Son Jesus is the Holy Ark that contains the presence of God, a presence that is a source of consolation, of total joy. John, in fact, leaps in Elizabeth's womb, just as David danced before the Ark. (HM 8-15-12)

God is man's home, in God there is God's space. And Mary, by uniting herself, united to God, does not distance herself from us. She does not go to an unknown galaxy, but whoever approaches God comes closer, for God is close to us all; and Mary, united to God, shares in the presence of God, is so close to us, to each one of us. (HM 8-15-12)

Mary, totally united to God, has a heart so big that all creation can enter this heart.... Mary is close, she can hear us, she can help us, she is close to every one of us. (HM 8-15-12)

In us there is room, let us open ourselves as Mary opened herself, saying: "Let your will be done, I am the servant of the Lord." By opening ourselves to God, we lose nothing. On the contrary, our life becomes rich and great. (HM 8-15-12)

Mary is the dawn and the splendor of the Church triumphant; she is the consolation and the hope of people still on the journey.... Let us entrust ourselves to her Motherly intercession, that she may obtain that he strengthen our faith in eternal life; may she help us to live in the best way the time that God has given us. (HM 8-15-12)

(Mary) is the "blessed among women" (Lk 1:42) — in the words of Saint Elizabeth's greeting. Her whole life was spent in the light of the Lord, within the radius of his name and of the face of God incarnate in Jesus, the "blessed fruit of her womb." This is how Luke's Gospel presents her to us. (HM 1-1-12)

Mary is the mother and model of the Church, who receives the divine Word in faith and offers herself to God as the "good soil" in which he can continue to accomplish his mystery of salvation. (HM 1-1-12)

The Angel, "appearing to her," does not call her by her earthly name, Mary, but by her divine name, as she has always been seen and characterized by God: "Full of grace — *gratia plena*," and the grace is none other than the love of God; thus, in the end, we can translate this word: "beloved" of God. (I 54)

The Mother of the Redeemer is held up as an image and model of holiness for every Christian and for the entire Church. (HM 5-1-11)

By her "yes" to God's call, the Virgin Mary manifested divine love among men. In this sense she, with her simplicity and maternal heart, continues to indicate the one Light and the one Truth: her Son, Jesus Christ, who is the definite answer to the question of the meaning of life. (HM 12-12-11)

Learn from the Mother of the Lord and our Mother to be humble and at the same time courageous, simple and prudent; meek and strong, not with the strength of the world but with the strength of the truth. (HM 10-23-11)

In contemplating the Virgin Mary we are granted another grace: the ability to see our own life too in depth. Yes, because our own daily existence, with its problems and hopes, receives light from the Mother of God, from her spiritual journey, from her destiny of glory: a journey and a destination than can and must become, in a certain way, our own journey and our own destination. (HM 8-15-11)

The New Testament tells us that the true ark of the covenant is a living, real person: it is the Virgin Mary. God does not dwell in a piece of furniture, he dwells in a person, in a heart: Mary, the One who carried in her womb the eternal Son of God made man, Jesus our Lord and Savior. (HM 8-15-11)

Christian piety rightly turns to Our Lady in the litanies in her honor, invoking her as *Foederis Arca,* that is, "the Ark of the Covenant," the Ark of God's presence, the Ark of the Covenant of love which God desired to establish with the whole of humanity, in Christ, once and for all. (HM 8-15-11)

Let us look to Mary: She opens us to hope, to a future full of joy and teaches us the way to achieve it: welcoming in faith: by welcoming her Son with faith; by never losing the friendship with him but letting ourselves be illuminated and guided by his word. (HM 8-15-11)

Outstanding among the saints is Mary, Mother of the Lord and mirror of all holiness. (D 22)

She is lowly: her only desire is to be the handmaid of the Lord (Lk 1:38, 48). She knows that she will only contribute to the salvation of the world if, rather than carrying out her own projects, she places herself completely at the disposal of God's initiatives. (D 22)

The Magnificat—a portrait, so to speak, of her soul—is entirely woven from threads of Holy Scripture, threads drawn from the Word of God. Here we see how completely at home Mary is with the Word of God, with ease she moves in and out of it. She speaks and thinks with the Word of God, the Word of God becomes her word, and her word issues from the Word of God. (D 22)

She is Queen of Heaven and earth. And is she really so remote from us? The contrary is true. Precisely because she is with God and in God, she is very close to each one of us. (I 61)

The words addressed by the crucified Lord to his disciple—to John and through him to all disciples of Jesus: "Behold, your mother!" (Jn 19:27)—are fulfilled anew in every generation. Mary has truly become the Mother of all believers. (D 23)

Men and women of every time and place have recourse to (Mary's) motherly kindness and her virginal purity and grace, in all their needs and aspirations, their joys and sorrows, their moments of loneliness and their common endeavors.... The testimonials of gratitude, offered to her from every continent and culture, are a recognition of that pure love which is not self-seeking but simply benevolent. (D 23)

The true stars of our life are the people who have lived good lives. They are lights of hope. Certainly, Jesus Christ is the true light, the sun that has risen above all the shadows of history. But to reach him we also need lights close by — people who shine with his light and so guide us along our way. Who more than Mary could be a star of hope for us? (s 25)

It is a duty of the Church to remember the greatness of Our Lady for the faith. (HM 8-15-12)

Mary does not appear in the accounts of Christ's resurrection, yet hers is, as it were, a continual, hidden presence: she is the Mother to which Jesus entrusted each of his disciples and the entire community. In particular we can see how Saint John and Saint Luke record the powerful, maternal presence of Mary. (HM 5-1-11)

THE LUMINOUS
MYSTERIES

THE FIRST LUMINOUS MYSTERY
The Baptism in the Jordan

SPIRITUAL CHILDHOOD

*Let the children come to me, do not
hinder them; for to such belongs the
kingdom of God.* —Mark 10:14

The Church of love is also the Church of truth, understood primarily as fidelity to the Gospel entrusted by the Lord Jesus to his followers. It was being made children of the same Father by the Spirit of truth that gave rise to Christian brotherhood: "For all who are led by the Spirit of God are sons of God" (Rom 8:14). (J 21)

Even before he does anything, the Christian already possesses a rich and fruitful interiority, given to him in the Sacraments of Baptism and Confirmation, an interiority which establishes him in an objective and original relationship of sonship with God. (J 120)

This is our greatest dignity: to be not merely images but also children of God ... we are adoptive sons in God's great family. (J 120)

God considers us his children, having raised us to a similar if not equal dignity to that of Jesus himself, the one true Son in the full sense. Our filial condition and trusting freedom in our relationship with the Father is given or restored to us in him. (J 120)

We are children of Abraham simply through faith in Christ. (J 141)

This journey toward humility, toward spiritual childhood is essential. It is necessary to overcome the attitude of arrogance that makes one say: I know better, in this my time of the twenty-first century, than what people could have known then. (C 71)

The Fathers developed the idea of God's birth in us through faith and baptism, in which the *Logos* comes to us ever anew, making us God's children. (J1 37)

The poor, the simple souls . . . Jesus would bless, because to them above all is granted access to the mystery of God (Lk 10:21). They represent the *poor of Israel*, the poor in general: God's first love. (J1 72)

"Let the children come to me; do not hinder them, for to such belongs the kingdom of God" . . . (Mk 10:13-16). The children serve Jesus as an example of the littleness before God that is necessary in order to pass through the "eye of a needle," the image that he used immediately afterward in the story of the rich young man (Mk 10:17-27). (J3 9)

"Children of God" . . . (are) all those who are willing to hear his call. (J3 175)

The tenderness, concern, and gentleness of God's kindness to us are so great that they remind us, pilgrims on earth, of a mother's love for her children. In fact, the biblical prophets also sometimes used this language that calls to mind the tenderness, intensity, and totality of God's love. (H 163)

God always excels all human love, as the Prophet Isaiah says: "Can a woman forget her suckling child, that she should have no compassion on the son of her womb? Even these may forget, yet I will never forget you" (Is 49:15). (H 163)

Holiness has its deepest root in the grace of baptism, in being grafted on to the Paschal Mystery of Christ, by which his Spirit is communicated to us, his very life as the Risen One. (H 240)

Here is the foundation of our peace: the certainty of contemplating in Jesus Christ the splendor of the face of God the Father, of being sons in the Son, and thus of having, on life's journey, the same security that a child feels in the arms of a loving and all-powerful Father. (HM 1-1-13)

In the sacrament of Baptism . . . is expressed the living and active presence of the Holy Spirit who, enriching the Church with new children, vitalizes and develops her, and we cannot but rejoice in this. (HM 1-13-13)

By his sacrifice, Jesus has opened for us the path to a profound relationship with God: in him we have become true adopted children and thus sharers in his kingship over the world. (HM 11-25-12)

Solemnly purified, Christians can regain a legitimate pride in their dignity as children of God, created in his image and redeemed by the precious blood of Jesus Christ, and they can experience his joy in order to share it with everyone, both near and far. (HM 10-7-12)

According to our faith, in deed, the Church is the Israel made universal, in which all become, through the Lord, children of Abraham. (HM 9-2-12)

The Church exercises her motherhood especially in the

sacrament of Baptism, when she generates God's children from water and the Holy Spirit, who cries out in each of them: "Abba, Father!" (Gal 4:6). (HM 1-1-12)

The breath of God is life. Now, the Lord breathes into our soul the new breath of life, the Holy Spirit, his most intimate essence, and in this way welcomes us into God's family. With Baptism and Confirmation this gift was given to us specifically, and with the sacraments of the Eucharist and Penance it is continuously repeated. (HM 6-12-11)

The everlasting God has entered our history and he remains present in a unique way in the person of Jesus, his incarnate Son, our Savior, who came down to earth to renew humanity radically and to free us from sin and death, to raise us to the dignity of God's children. (HM 12-31-11)

"Go therefore and make disciples of all nations, baptizing them in the name of the Father and of the Son and of the Holy Spirit" (Mt 28:19). The Baptism that Jesus's disciples have been administering since he spoke those words is an entrance into the Master's own Baptism—into the reality that he anticipated by means of it. That is the way to become a Christian. (J2 23)

The love that endures "to the end" (Jn 13:1), which the Lord fulfilled on the Cross in praying for his enemies, shows us the essence of the Father. He is this love. Because Jesus brings it to completion, he is entirely "Son," and he invites us to become "sons" according to this criterion. (J2 136)

First of all, God is our Father in the sense that he is our Creator. We belong to him because he has created us. "Being" as such comes from him and is consequently good; it derives from God. This is especially true of human beings. (J2 137)

The idea that God has created each individual human being is essential to the Bible's image of man. Every human being is unique, and willed as such by God. Every individual is known to him. In this sense, by virtue of creation itself man is the "child" of God in a special way, and God is his true Father. (J2 138)

The Fathers of the Church say that when God created man "in his image," he looked toward the Christ who was to come, and created man according to the image of the "new Adam," the man who is the criterion of the human.... He wants to draw all of us into his humanity and so into his Sonship, into his total belonging to God. (J2 138)

We are not ready-made children of God from the start, but we are meant to become so increasingly by growing more and more deeply in communion with Jesus. Our sonship turns out to be identical with following Christ. To name God as Father thus becomes a summons to us: to live as a "child," as a son or daughter. (J2 138)

The word *father* is an invitation to live from our awareness of this reality. (J2 138)

We see that to be God's child is not a matter of dependency, but rather of standing in the relation of love that sustains man's existence and gives it meaning and grandeur. (J2 139)

Jesus alone was fully entitled to say "my Father," because he alone is truly God's only-begotten Son, of one substance with the Father. By contrast, the rest of us have to say "our Father." Only within the "we" of the disciples can we call God "Father," because only through communion with Jesus Christ do we truly become "children of God." (J2 140 & 141)

We have the right and the duty to ask for what we need. We know that if even earthly fathers give their children good things when they ask for them, God will not refuse us the good things that he alone can give (Lk 11:9-13). (J2 151)

The Lord wants to lead us from foolish cleverness toward true wisdom; he wants to teach us to discern the real good.... The next life only brings to light the truth already present in this life. (J2 215)

If Christians consider the crossing of the Red Sea as a prefiguring of Baptism, there in the immediate foreground is the symbolism of death: It becomes an image of the mystery of the Cross. In order to be reborn, man must first enter with Christ into the "Red Sea," plunge with him down into death, in order thus to attain new life with the risen Lord. (J2 239)

Rebirth—to put it in another way—involves the creative power of God's Spirit, but it also requires the sacrament of the maternal womb of the receiving and welcoming Church. (J2 240)

Spirit and water, heaven and earth, Christ and the Church, belong together. And this is how "rebirth" happens. In the sacrament, water stands for the maternal earth, the holy Church, which welcomes creation into herself and stands in place of it. (J2 240)

To be a son is to be in relation: it is a relational concept. It involves giving up the autonomy that is closed in upon itself; it includes what Jesus means by saying that we have to become like children. (J2 343)

God is our Father and loves us, even when his silence remains incomprehensible. (D 21)

The Church rejoices in each "new creation" (Gal 6:15, 2 Cor 5:17) incorporated by Baptism into her living Body. (CV 30)

"Blessed are the pure in heart, for they shall see God" (Mt 5:8). Purity of heart is what enables us to see. Therein consists the ultimate simplicity that opens up our life to Jesus's will to reveal.... Our will has to become a filial will. (J2 343)

While we have different earthly fathers, we all come from one single Father, who is the measure and source of all fatherhood. As Saint Paul says: "I bow my knees before the Father, from whom every fatherhood in heaven and on earth is named" (Eph 3:14-15). (J2 141)

God's fatherhood is more real than human fatherhood, because he is the ultimate source of our being; because he has thought and willed us from all eternity; because he gives us our true paternal home, which is eternal. (J2 141 & 142)

There is no true prayer without the presence of the Spirit within us . . . learn to speak to the Father as children in the Holy Spirit. (J 121 & 122)

Through Baptism each child is inserted into a gathering of friends who never abandon him in life or in death, because these companions are God's family, which in itself bears the promise of eternity. (I 13)

THE SECOND LUMINOUS MYSTERY
The Wedding at Cana

MARRIAGE & FAMILY LIFE

Every sound tree bears good fruit, but the bad
tree bears evil fruit. —Matthew 7:17

Thanks to the faith and apostolic commitment of the lay faithful, of families, of spouses. . . . Christianity has reached our generation. It could not grow only due to the Apostles who announced it. In order to take root in people's land and develop actively, the commitment of these families, these spouses, these Christian communities, of these lay faithful was necessary. (J 148 & 149)

How important the action of Christian spouses is! When they are supported by the faith and by a strong spirituality, their courageous commitment for the Church and in the Church becomes natural. (J 149)

Every home can transform itself into a little church. Not only in the sense that in them must reign the typical Christian love made of altruism and of reciprocal care, but still more in the sense that the whole of family life, based on faith, is called to revolve around the singular lordship of Jesus Christ. (J 149)

Not by chance does Paul compare, in the Letter to the Ephesians, the matrimonial relationship to the spousal communion that happens between Christ and the Church . . . the Church, in reality, is the family of God. (J 149)

The Trinity is truly perfect communion! How the world would change if relations were always lived in families, in parishes, and in every other community by following the example of the three divine Persons, in whom each lives not only *with* the other, but *for* the other and *in* the other! (C 190)

The only laws in conformity with equity are those that protect the sacredness of human life and reject the licitness of abortion, euthanasia, and bold genetic experimentation, those laws that respect the dignity of marriage between a man and a woman, that are inspired by a correct secularism of the State—a secularism that always entails the safeguard of religious freedom. (C 208)

The theology and spirituality of Christian marriage have considerably deepened the analogy with the spousal relationship of Christ and his Church. (C 213)

I believe we must all try together to find new ways of bringing the Gospel to the contemporary world, of proclaiming Christ anew and of implanting the faith.... For the Church and especially for us Pastors, for parents and for educators, young people constitute a living appeal to faith. (G 94)

The number of young people from broken families is on the rise.... Many of the ideas put forward by modern society lead nowhere, and, unfortunately, very many young people end in the quicksand of alcohol and drugs or in the clutches of extremist groups. (G 97)

We see the threat to families...how important it is that the family live as the primary cell of society, that children be able to grow in an atmosphere of communion between generations, so that continuity between the present, past and future will endure and that the continuity of values will be lasting: this is what makes it possible to build communion in a country. (G 98 & 99)

Christian spouses can make a journey of holiness sustained by the grace of the sacrament of Marriage. (H 136)

It is often the woman . . . who with her religious sensitivity, delicacy, and gentleness succeeds in persuading her husband to follow a path of faith. I am thinking with gratitude of the many women who, day after day, illuminate their families with their witness of Christian life. (H 136)

May the Lord's Spirit still inspire holiness in Christian spouses today, to show the world the beauty of marriage lived in accordance with the Gospel values: love, tenderness, reciprocal help, fruitfulness in begetting and in raising children, openness and solidarity to the world, and participation in the life of the Church. (H 136 & 137)

From the example of Saint Joseph we all receive a strong invitation to carry out with fidelity, simplicity and modesty the task that Providence has entrusted to us. I think especially of fathers and mothers of families, and I pray that they will always be able to appreciate the beauty of a simple and industrious life. (I 41)

Matrimony is a Gospel in itself, a Good News for the world of today, especially the dechristianized world. The union of a man and a woman, their becoming "one flesh" in charity, in fruitful and indissoluble love, is a sign that speaks of God with a force and an eloquence which in our days has become greater. (HM 10-7-12)

The Church sees in the family a most important value that must be defended from any attack that aims to undermine its solidity and call its very existence into question. (I 25)

Marriage is linked to faith, but not in a general way. Marriage, as a union of faithful and indissoluble love, is based upon the grace that comes from the triune God who in Christ loves us with a faithful love, even to the Cross.... There is a clear link between the crisis in faith and the crisis in marriage. (HM 10-7-12)

Parents carry out an educational mission for their children in the family. (HM 7-15-12)

Raising children is very demanding and at times taxes our human capability, which is always limited. However, educating becomes a marvelous mission if it is carried out in collaboration with God who is the first and true educator of every human being. (HM 1-8-12)

What are the "springs of salvation"? They are the Word of God and the sacraments. Adults are the first who should nourish themselves at these sources, so as to be able to guide those who are younger in their development. (HM 1-8-12)

It is very important for you parents, and also for the godparents, to believe strongly in the presence and in the action of the Holy Spirit, to invoke him and to welcome him within you, through prayer and through the sacraments. It is he, in fact, who illumines the mind and warms the heart of the educator so that he or she can pass on the knowledge and love of Jesus. (HM 1-8-12)

Prayer is the first condition for teaching because by praying we prepare ourselves to leave the initiative to God, to entrust children to him, who knows them before and better than we, and who knows perfectly what their true good is. (HM 1-8-12)

Prayer and the sacraments obtain for us that light of truth thanks to which we are able to be at once tender and strong, gentle and firm, silent and communicative at the right time, admonishing and correcting in the right way. (HM 1-8-12)

Let us therefore all invoke the Holy Spirit together so that he may come down upon these children in abundance, consecrate them in the image of Jesus Christ and always go with them on their journey through life. (HM 1-8-12)

The fruitfulness of the womb has always been associated with God's blessing. The Mother of God is the first of the blessed, and it is she who bears the blessing; she is the woman who received Jesus into herself and brought him forth for the whole human family. (HM 1-1-12)

In the face of the shadows that obscure the horizon of today's world, to assume responsibility for educating young people in knowledge of the truth, in fundamental values and virtues, is to look to the future with hope. And in this commitment to a holistic education, formation in justice and peace has a place. (HM 1-1-12)

Every pathway of authentic religious formation guides the person, from the most tender age, to know God, to love him and to do his will. (HM 1-1-12)

Christian families are a decisive resource for education in the faith, for the upbuilding of the church as a communion and for her missionary presence in the most diverse situations in life. (HM 6-5-11)

The Christian family is a special sign of the presence and love of Christ. . . . It is called to give a specific and irreplaceable contribution to evangelization. (HM 6-5-11)

Christian parents, commit yourselves always to teach your children to pray, and pray with them; draw them close to the Sacraments, especially to the Eucharist. (HM 6- 5-11)

In the intimacy of the home do not be afraid to read the sacred Scriptures, illuminating family life with the light of faith and praising God as Father. Be like a little Upper Room like that of Mary and the disciples, in which to live unity, communion and prayer! (HM 6-5-11)

Dear families, be courageous! Do not give in to that secularized mentality which proposes living together as a preparation, or even as a substitute, for marriage! Show by the witness of your lives that it is possible, like Christ, to live without reserve, and do not be afraid to make a commitment to another person! (HM 6-5-11)

Without trust in God, without trust in Christ ... the family cannot survive. We see this today. Only faith in Christ and only sharing the faith of the Church saves the family; and on the other hand, only if this family is saved can the Church survive. (I 26)

Dear families, rejoice in fatherhood and motherhood! Openness to life is a sign of openness to the future, confidence in the future, just as respect for the natural moral law frees people, rather than demeaning them! The good of the family is also the good of the Church. (HM 6-5-11)

The family of Nazareth presents a school of Christian life. (HM 10-23-11)

I would also like to encourage and bless the efforts of all those, priests and lay people, who are involved in the preparation of Christian couples for marriage and the family, in order to give an evangelical and competent response to the many contemporary challenges in the area of the family and of life. (HM 10-9-11)

In our era of restlessness and lack of commitment, when so many people lose their way and their grounding, when loving fidelity in marriage and friendship has become so fragile and short-lived, when in our need we cry out like the disciples on the road to Emmaus: "Lord, stay with us, for it is almost evening and darkness is all around us" (Lk 24:29), in this present era, the risen Lord gives us a place of refuge, a place of light, hope and confidence, a place of rest and security. (HM 9-22-11)

A Eucharistic spirituality is the true antidote to the individualism and selfishness that often mark daily life. It leads to the rediscovery of giving freely, to the centrality of relationships, starting with the family, and pays special attention to alleviating the wounds of broken families. (HM 9-11-11)

From her very inception, the Church that emerged, and continues to emerge, has attached fundamental importance to defending the family as the core of all social order. (J2 121)

Corresponding to the image of a monotheistic God is a monogamous marriage. Marriage based on exclusive and definitive love becomes the icon of the relationship between God and his people and vice versa. God's way of loving becomes the measure of human love. (D 7)

The Encyclical *Humanae Vitae* emphasizes both the unitive and the procreative meaning of sexuality, thereby locating at the foundation of society the married couple, man and woman, who accept one another mutually, in distinction and in complementarity: a couple, therefore, that is open to life. (CV 7)

This is not a question of purely individual morality: *Humanae Vitae* indicates the strong links between life and social ethics. (CV 7)

In economically developed countries, legislation contrary to life is very widespread, and it has already shaped moral attitudes and praxis, contributing to the spread of an anti-birth mentality; frequent attempts are made to export this mentality to other States as if it were a form of cultural progress. (CV 14)

If personal and social sensitivity towards the acceptance of a new life is lost, then other forms of acceptance that are valuable for society also wither away. The acceptance of life strengthens moral fiber and makes people capable of mutual help. (CV 14)

It is irresponsible to view sexuality merely as a source of pleasure, and likewise to regulate it through strategies of mandatory birth control. In either case materialistic ideas and policies are at work, and individuals are ultimately subjected to various forms of violence. Against such policies, there is a need to defend the primary competence of the family in the area of sexuality, as opposed to the State and its restrictive policies. (CV 24)

Smaller and at times minuscule families run the risk of impoverishing social relations, and failing to ensure effective forms of solidarity. These situations are symptomatic of scant confidence in the future and moral weariness. (CV 25)

It is becoming a social and even economic necessity once more to hold up to future generations the beauty of marriage and the family, and the fact that these institutions correspond to the deepest needs and dignity of the person. (CV 25)

States are called to enact policies promoting the centrality and the integrity of the family founded on marriage between a man and woman, the primary vital cell of society. (CV 25)

The sacramental love of spouses unites them spiritually in "one flesh" (Gen 2:24; Mt 19:5, Eph 5:31) and makes out of the two a real and relational unity. (CV 30)

THE THIRD LUMINOUS MYSTERY
The Proclamation of God

THE KINGDOM OF GOD

"Yes, I am a king. I was born for this, I came into the world for this: to bear witness to the truth; and all who are on the side of truth listen to my voice." —John 18:37

After Christ's Passion and Resurrection, this sign was to be made clear: the universal character of the Apostles' mission was to become explicit. Christ would send the Apostles "to the whole creation" (Mk 16:15), to "all nations" (Mt 28:19; Lk 24:47), "to the ends of the earth" (Acts 1:8). And this mission continues. (J 15)

(Nathanael) answers with a clear and beautiful confession of faith: "Rabbi, you are the Son of God! You are the King of Israel!" (Jn 1:49). In this confession is conveyed a first important step in the journey of attachment to Jesus. (J 98)

The growth of the universal dimension of the Church . . . is not restricted to one specific culture but is comprised of all the cultures of the world that must be open to Christ and find in him their goal. (C 75)

Mary is to bear a child, to whom the angel assigns the titles "Son of the Most High" and "Son of God." Moreover, it is promised that God, the Lord, will give him the throne of his father David. He will rule over the house of Jacob forever, and his kingdom (his reign) will have no end. (J1 28 & 29)

We Christians know and gratefully acknowledge that God did indeed carry out his promise. The kingship of Jesus,

Son of David, stretches "from sea to sea," from continent to continent, from one century to another. (J1 32)

The kingdom that Jesus proclaimed, the kingdom of God, is of another kind. It applies not just to the Mediterranean region and not just to a particular era. It applies to man in the depths of his being, and it opens him toward the true God. The peace of Jesus is a peace that the world cannot give (Jn 14:27). (J1 78)

In the kingdom of Jesus Christ there are no distinctions of race and origin. In him and through him, humanity is united, yet without losing any of the richness of variety. (J1 96)

Paul emphasizes that the risen Christ has conquered all the powers and forces in the heavens, and that he reigns over the entire universe. (J1 101)

The mystery of the Cross (is) a mystery that is inseparably linked with Jesus's kingship.... It is true: God disturbs our comfortable day-to-day existence. Jesus's kingship goes hand in hand with his Passion. (J1 102 & 103)

The present "world" has to disappear; it must be changed into God's world. That is precisely what Jesus's mission is, into which the disciples are taken up: leading "the world" away from the condition of man' alienation from God and from himself, so that it can become God's world once more and so that man can become fully himself again by becoming one with God. (J3 101)

Whereas John the Baptist had called people to conversion in the face of the threat of judgment, Jesus, as the messenger of joy, proclaimed that God's lordship and unconditional readiness to forgive were close at hand, that the dominion of God's goodness and mercy had arrived. (J3 118)

Only through faith in the Crucified One, in him who was robbed of all worldly power and thereby exalted, does the new community arise, the new manner of God's dominion in the world. (J3 171)

All the way to the Cross — all the way to the inscription above the Cross — is the kingdom of God, the new kingship represented by Jesus. And this kingship is centered on truth. (J3 194)

The kingship proclaimed by Jesus, at first in parables and then at the end quite openly before the earthly judge, is none other than the kingship of truth. The inauguration of this kingship is man's true liberation. (J3 194)

Jesus is "exalted." The Cross is his throne, from which he draws the world to himself. From this place of total self-sacrifice, from this place of truly divine love, he reigns as the true king in his own way — a way that neither Pilate nor the members of the Sanhedrin had been able to comprehend. (J3 211 & 212)

The final command to those sent out by Jesus is universal: "All authority in heaven and on earth has been given to me. Go therefore and make disciples of all nations" (Mt 28:18-19). (J3 278)

Jesus will come again to judge the living and the dead and to establish God's kingdom definitively in the world. (J3 279)

We are concerned for the state of the world and we are asking: "Where do I find standards to live by, what are the criteria that govern responsible cooperation in building the present and the future of our world? On whom can I rely?"... Our journey is not over until we meet the One who has the power to establish that universal Kingdom of justice and peace to which all people aspire. (G 37)

God does not enter into competition with earthly powers in this world. He does not marshal his divisions alongside other divisions. God did not send twelve legions of angels to assist Jesus in the Garden of Olives (Mt 26:53). He contrasts the noisy and ostentatious power of this world with the defenseless power of love. (G 51)

The Church invites us to celebrate the Lord Jesus as King of the Universe. She calls us to look to the future, or more properly into the depths, to the ultimate goal of history, which will be the definitive and eternal kingdom of Christ. (HM 11-25-12)

(Jesus Christ) was with the Father in the beginning, when the world was created, and he will fully manifest his lordship at the end of time, when he will judge all mankind. (HM 11-25-12)

The author of the Book of Revelation broadens his gaze to include Jesus's second coming to judge mankind and to establish forever his divine kingdom, and he reminds us that conversion, as a response to God's grace, is the condition for the establishment of this kingdom (Rev 1:7). (HM 11-25-12)

We invoke the kingdom daily in the prayer of the "Our Father" with the words "Thy kingdom come"; in effect we say to Jesus: Lord, make us yours, live in us, gather together a scattered and suffering humanity, so that in you all may be subjected to the Father of mercy and love. (HM 11-25-12)

What makes the Church catholic is the fact that Christ in his saving mission embraces all humanity. While during his earthly life Jesus's mission was limited to the Jewish people, "to the lost sheep of the house of Israel" (Mt 15:24), from the beginning it was meant to bring the light of the Gospel to all peoples and lead all nations into the kingdom of God. (HM 11-24-12)

The Blessed Sacrament is carried in procession through the streets of the cities and villages, to show that the Risen Christ walks in our midst and guides us towards the Kingdom of Heaven. (HM 6-23-11)

The proclamation of God's Kingdom, of God's unlimited goodness, must first of all bring healing to broken hearts. By nature, man is a being in relation. But if the fundamental relationship, the relationship with God, is disturbed, then all the rest is disturbed as well. (HM 4-21-11)

Christ reigns from the Cross and, with his arms open wide, he embraces all the peoples of the world and draws them into unity. Through the Cross, he breaks down the walls of division, he reconciles us with each other and with the Father. (HM 11-20-11)

His Kingdom can be threatened in our hearts. There God comes face to face with our freedom. We—and we alone—can prevent him from reigning over us and consequently obstructing his Lordship over our families, society and history. (HM 11-20-11)

No kingdom of this world is the Kingdom of God, the total condition of mankind's salvation. Earthly kingdoms remain earthly human kingdoms, and anyone who claims to be able to establish the perfect world is the willing dupe of Satan and plays the world right into his hands. (J2 43 & 44)

What did Jesus actually bring, if not world peace, universal prosperity, and a better world? What has he brought? The answer is very simple: God. He has brought God....It is this God, the God of Abraham, Isaac and Jacob, the true God, whom he has brought to the nations of the earth. (J2 44)

The core content of the Gospel is this: The Kingdom of God is at hand. A milestone is set up in the flow of time; something new takes place. And an answer to this gift is demanded of man: conversion and faith. The center of this announcement is the message that God's Kingdom is at hand. This announcement is the actual core of Jesus's words and works. (J2 47)

Jesus himself is the Kingdom; the Kingdom is not a thing, it is not a geographical dominion like worldly kingdoms. It is a person; it is he. On this interpretation, the term "Kingdom of God" is itself a veiled Christology . . . he is God's presence. (J2 49)

The "Kingdom of God" is not to be found on any map. It is not a kingdom after the fashion of worldly kingdoms; it is located in man's inner being. It grows and radiates outward from that inner space. (J2 50)

The phrase "Kingdom of heaven" is not a one-sided declaration of something "beyond": it speaks of God, who is as much in this world as he is beyond it—who infinitely transcends our world, but is also totally interior to it. (J2 55)

When Jesus speaks of the Kingdom of God, he is quite simply proclaiming God, and proclaiming him to be the living God, who is able to act concretely in the world and in history and is even now so acting. He is telling us: "God exists" and "God is really God," which means that he holds in his hands the threads of the world. (J2 55)

The divine lordship, God's dominion over the world and over history, transcends the moment, indeed transcends and reaches beyond the whole of history. Its inner dynamism carries history beyond itself. And yet it is at the same time something belonging absolutely to the present. (J2 57)

Jesus sits on the *cathedra* of Moses. But he does so not after the manner of teachers who are trained for the job in a school; he sits there as the greater Moses, who broadens the Covenant to include all nations. (J2 66)

Where God is absent, nothing can be good. Where God is not seen, man and the world fall to ruin. This is what the Lord means when he says to "seek first his Kingdom and his righteousness, and all these things shall be yours as well" (Mt 6:33). These words establish an order of priorities for human action, for how we approach everyday life. (J2 145)

With the petition "thy Kingdom come"... the first and essential thing is a listening heart, so that God, not we, may reign. The Kingdom of God comes by way of a listening heart. That is its path. And that is what we must pray for again and again. (J2 146)

For Jesus himself and for his followers, miracles of healing are thus a subordinate element within the overall range of his activity, which is concerned with something deeper, with nothing less than the "Kingdom of God": his becoming Lord in us and in the world. (J2 176)

God offers us a complete vision of man in history: fascinated by Wisdom, he seeks it and finds it in Christ, leaving everything for him and receiving in exchange the priceless gift of the Kingdom of God. (1 83)

The Kingdom arrives in the person of Christ. In pointing to the Kingdom, the parables thus point to him as the Kingdom's true form. (J2 187)

(The) image of Christ the Good Shepherd is a Gospel of Christ the King, an image that sheds light upon the kingship of Christ. (J2 272)

It is true, of course, that the title Messiah, "King of the Jews," is placed over the Cross—publicly displayed before the whole world. And it is permissible to place it there—in the three languages of the world of that time (Jn 19:19)—because now there is no longer any chance of its being misunderstood. The Cross is his throne. (J2 321)

This one thing that is the object of man's many wishes and hopes also finds expression in the second petition of the Our Father: Thy Kingdom come. The "Kingdom of God" is life in abundance—precisely because it is not just private "happiness," not individual joy, but the world having attained its rightful form, the unity of God and the world. (J2 353)

Man needs God, otherwise he remains without hope.... A "Kingdom of God" accomplished without God—a kingdom therefore of man alone—inevitably ends up as the "perverse end" of all things. (S 12)

In every community love one another; do not be divided but live as brothers and sisters so that the world may believe that Jesus is alive in his Church and that the Kingdom of God is at hand. (HM 7-15-12)

This is the meaning behind our journey: to serve the kingship of God in the world...this is the mystery of God's call, the mystery of vocation. It is part of the life of every Christian. (G 46)

Although the Kingdom of God bursts definitively into history with Jesus's Resurrection, it has not yet come about fully. The final victory will only be won with the Second Coming of the Lord, which we await with patient hope. (HM 1-25-12)

From the first moment of his salvific activity, Jesus of Nazareth strives to gather together the People of God. Even if his preaching is always an appeal for personal conversion, in reality he continually aims to build the People of God whom he came to bring together, purify, and save. (J 8)

The Church, despite all the human frailties that mark her historical profile, is revealed as a marvelous creation of love, brought into being to bring Christ close to every man and every woman who truly desires to meet him, until the end of time. (J 19)

God is one, there is no other; there are no gods other than the Lord.... The epochal upheavals and succession of great powers are under the supreme domination of God; no earthly power can stand in his stead. (HM 10-16-11)

THE FOURTH LUMINOUS MYSTERY
The Transfiguration

THE LIGHT OF CHRIST

*I am the light of the world; anyone who
follows me will not be walking in the dark;
he will have the light of life.* —John 8:12

This is how Jesus's love for us reaches us: by the pouring out
of his own Blood for our salvation! The Christian, pausing
in contemplation before this "excess" of love, cannot but
wonder what the proper response is. And I think each one
of us, always and over and over again, must ask himself
this. (J 73)

The mystery of the Cross stands at the center of the history
of salvation as recounted in the Old Testament; it shows
that Jesus, Crucified and Risen, is truly the goal of all this
history. (J 136)

We ourselves have this very deep certainty that Christ is the
answer and that without the concrete God, the God with
the Face of Christ, the world destroys itself. (I 32)

The loftiest concepts of God never reach his true grandeur:
they always fall short of it.... It is easier for us to say what
God is not rather than to say what he truly is. Only through
these images can we intuit his true Face; moreover, this Face
of God is very concrete: it is Jesus Christ. (C 29)

The path of dialogue consists precisely in being close to God
in Christ, in a deep encounter with him, in the experience of
the truth which opens us to the light and helps us reach out

to others with the light of truth, the light of love.... Then the heart is enlarged and can see and also illumine reason so that it perceives God's beauty. (C 30)

Christ is true man and true God, and in being the true man-God, he is only one Person, the synthesis between Creation and the Creator, in whose human words we hear the voice of the Word of God himself. (C 35)

As a result of the Incarnation, matter is seen to have become divine, is seen as the habitation of God. It is a new vision of the world and of material reality. God became flesh, and flesh became truly the habitation of God, whose glory shines in the human Face of Christ. (C 101)

The Transfiguration ... prefigures the Resurrection. (C 155)

Christ is the Door that leads to Heaven. (C 181)

The individual truths of faith illuminate each other and, in their total and unitive vision, the harmony of God's plan of salvation and the centrality of the mystery of Christ become evident. (C 212)

With Jesus "the fullness of time" had come ... with him the decisive hour of world history had dawned: he is the new Adam, who once again comes "from God"—but in a more radical way than the first Adam, not merely breathed into being by God, but truly God's "Son." (J1 10)

The God who *is,* is the saving God, now present. The revelation of God's name, which began in the burning bush, comes to completion in Jesus (Jn 17:26). (J1 30)

Christ, the incarnate Son, is—so to speak—God's first thought, preceding all creation, which is ordered toward him and proceeds from him. He is both the beginning and the goal of the new creation that was initiated with the resurrection. (J1 71)

The "glory" of God is real, God *is* glorious, and this is truly a reason for joy: there *is* truth, there *is* goodness, there *is* beauty. It is there—in God. (J1 74)

The darkness in which mankind is groping needs to be illuminated. Jesus taught us how this can be done: "If you continue in my word, you are truly my disciples; and you will know the truth, and the truth will make you free." The incarnate Word, Word of Truth, makes us free and directs our freedom toward the good. (I 28)

Human nature assumed by God—as revealed in God's only-begotten Son—is greater than all the powers of the material world, greater than the entire universe. (J1 102)

From the Cross, the one God becomes visible to the nations; in the Son they will recognize the Father, that is to say, the one God, who revealed himself in the burning bush. (J3 19 & 20)

The light of Jesus can illumine and overcome the darkness. (J3 69)

In Jesus, God gives himself entirely into the world of mankind: whoever sees Jesus sees the Father (Jn 14:9). . . . God has entered our very being. In him God is truly "God-with-us." (J3 91 & 92)

As the risen Lord, he is now in the fullest sense the shepherd who leads, through death, to the path of life. The Good Shepherd does both: he offers up his life, and he goes before. Indeed, the offering up of his life *is* the going before. It is through these actions that he leads us. (J3 151)

"Redemption" in the fullest sense can only consist in the truth becoming recognizable. And it becomes recognizable when God becomes recognizable. He becomes recognizable in Jesus Christ. In Christ, God entered the world and set up the criterion of truth in the midst of history. (J3 194)

The darkness and irrationality of sin and the holiness of God, too dazzling for our eyes, come together in the Cross, transcending our power of understanding. And yet in the message of the New Testament, and in the proof of that message in the lives of the saints, the great mystery has become radiant light. (J3 240)

Is it not what seems so small that is truly great? Does not a ray of light issue from Jesus, growing brighter across the centuries, that could not come from any mere man and through which the light of God truly shines into the world? (J3 276 & 277)

The disciples undoubtedly spoke of Jesus's return, but first and foremost they bore witness to the fact that he is alive now, that he is Life itself, in whom we, too, come alive (Jn 14:19). (J3 279)

Like the Magi, all believers ... have been called to set out on the journey of life in search of truth, justice and love. We must seek this star, we must follow it. The ultimate goal of the journey can be found only through an encounter with Christ, an encounter which cannot take place without faith. (G 30)

Open the doors of your freedom to his merciful love! Share your joys and pains with Christ, and let him enlighten your minds with his light and touch your hearts with his grace. (G 36)

We discover the joy of belonging to a family as vast as the world, including Heaven and earth, the past, the present, the future and every part of the earth. In this great band of pilgrims we walk side by side with Christ, we walk with the star that enlightens our history. (G 55)

Jesus Christ is God's last word — in him God said all, giving and expressing himself. More than himself, God cannot express or give.... Thus there is no loftier Gospel, there is no other Church to await. (H 45)

The Incarnation is the greatest and most beautiful work of the entire history of salvation...(it) is God's original idea of ultimately uniting with himself the whole of creation, in the Person and Flesh of the Son. (H 88)

God is love and it is only if one opens oneself to this love, totally and with total trust, and lets it become one's sole guide in life, that all things are transfigured, true peace and true joy found and one is able to radiate it. (H 163)

Holiness is not a very difficult action of ours but means exactly this "openness": opening the windows of our soul to let in God's light, without forgetting God, because it is precisely in opening oneself to his light that one finds strength, one finds the joy of the redeemed. (H 205)

I would like to ask all to open themselves to the action of the Holy Spirit, who transforms our life, to be, we too, like small pieces in the great mosaic of holiness that God continues to create in history, so that the face of Christ may shine out in the fullness of its splendor. (H 243)

Proclaim Christ anew in places where the light of faith has been weakened, in places where the fire of God is more like smoldering cinders, crying out to be stirred up, so that they can become a living flame that gives light and heat. (HM 10-28-12)

The great star, the true supernova that leads us on, is Christ himself. He is as it were the explosion of God's love, which causes the great white light of his heart to shine upon the world. (HM 1-6-12)

All things proceed from God, from the omnipotence of his Triune Love, incarnate in Jesus. Christ's heart is steeped in this Love; therefore he can thank and praise God even in the face of betrayal and violence, and in this way changes things, people and the world. (HM 6-23-11)

The words "Jesus is Lord" can be interpreted in two ways. They mean: Jesus is God, and, at the same time: God is Jesus. The Holy Spirit illuminated this reciprocity: Jesus has divine dignity and God has the human face of Jesus. (HM 6-12-11)

God is not distant from man but reached down to him and became flesh (Jn 1:14) so that man might understand where the solid foundation of all things, the fulfillment of his deepest yearnings lies: in Christ. (HM 12-15-11)

In the world's eyes it sometimes seems impossible to spend one's whole life in a monastery but in fact a whole life barely suffices to enter into this union with God, into this essential and profound Reality which is Jesus Christ. (HM 10-23-11)

The new and eternal life is the fruit of the tree of the Cross, a tree that blossoms and bears fruit from the light and power that radiate from the sun of God. (HM 11-3-11)

Jesus's teaching is not the product of human learning, of whatever kind. It originates from immediate contact with the Father, from "face to face" dialogue—from the vision of the one who rests close to the Father's heart. It is the Son's word. (J2 7)

(Jesus) himself is the treasure; communion with him is the pearl of great price. (J2 61)

Anyone who honestly and passionately searches for truth is on the way to Christ....To "hunger and thirst for righteousness"—that is the path that lies open to everyone; that is the way that finds its destination in Jesus Christ. (J2 91 & 92)

The figure of Jesus is the mirror in which we come to know who God is and what he is like: through the Son we find the Father. At the Last Supper, when Philip asks Jesus to "show us the Father," Jesus says, "He who sees me sees the Father" (Jn 14:8). (J2 137)

The promise to Moses is fulfilled superabundantly, in the overflowingly lavish way in which God is accustomed to bestow his gifts. The One who has come is more than Moses, more than a prophet. He is the Son. And that is why grace and truth now come to light, not in order to destroy the Law, but to fulfill it. (J2 236)

There is only one Shepherd. The Logos who became man in Jesus is the Shepherd of all men, for all have been created through the one Word; however scattered they may be, yet as coming from him and bound toward him they are one. However widely scattered they are, all people can become one through the true Shepherd. (J2 284)

The Transfiguration is a prayer event; it displays visibly what happens when Jesus talks with his Father: the profound interpenetration of his being with God, which then becomes pure light. In his oneness with the Father, Jesus is himself "light from light." (J2 310)

Jesus shines from within; he does not simply receive light, but he himself is light from light. Yet Jesus's garment of white light at the Transfiguration speaks of our future as well. (J2 310)

"I am the Bread of Life," "the Light of the World," "the Door," "the Good Shepherd," "the Resurrection and the Life," "the Way, the Truth, and the Life"... all these images are variations on the single theme, that Jesus has come so that human beings may have life, and have it in abundance (Jn 10:10). (J2 353)

Jesus himself is the truth.... Discover Christ again, and so find the centrality of faith again. (J3 59 & L 232)

In the Church, in God's word, in the celebration of the sacraments, in the Sacrament of Confession with the forgiveness that we receive, in the celebration of the Blessed Eucharist where the Lord gives himself into our hands and hearts, we touch the light. (HM 12-11-11)

THE FIFTH LUMINOUS MYSTERY
The Institution of the Eucharist

THE HOLY EUCHARIST

"He who eats my flesh and drinks my blood has eternal life, and I will raise him up at the last day."—John 6:54

In the Eucharist, Jesus nourishes us, he unites us with himself, with his Father, with the Holy Spirit, and with one another. This network of unity that embraces the world is an anticipation of the future world in our time. (J 18)

"Communion" is truly the Good News, the remedy given to us by the Lord to fight the loneliness that threatens everyone today, the precious gift that makes us feel welcomed and beloved by God, in the unity of his People gathered in the name of the Trinity; it is the light that makes the Church shine forth like a beacon raised among the peoples. (J 18 & 19)

Saint Paul said: "Because there is one bread, we who are many are one body" (1 Cor 10:17). In the same Eucharist, Christ gives us his Body and makes us his Body. Concerning this, Saint Paul said to the Galatians: "You are all one in Christ" (Gal 3:28). (J 126)

We are in danger of reappraising the Eucharistic reality, that is, of considering the Eucharist almost as a rite of communion, of socialization alone, forgetting all too easily that the Risen Christ is really present in the Eucharist with his Risen Body. (C 200)

(Jesus) called himself the true bread come down from heaven, the true nourishment that we need in order to be fully ourselves. This is the food that gives us true life, eternal life. (J1 68)

For the infant Church, "Palm Sunday" was not a thing of the past. Just as the Lord entered the Holy City that day on a donkey, so too the Church saw him coming again and again in the humble form of bread and wine. (J3 10)

The Church greets the Lord in the Holy Eucharist as the one who is coming now, the one who has entered into her midst. At the same time, she greets him as the one who continues to come, the one who leads us toward his coming. (J3 11)

From her earliest days, the Church has understood the words of consecration not simply as a kind of quasi-magical command, but as part of her praying in and with Jesus; as a central part of the praise and thanksgiving through which God's earthly gift is given to us anew in the form of Jesus's body and blood. (J3 128)

God's bountiful distribution of gifts takes on a radical quality when the Son communicates and distributes himself in the form of bread. (J3 129)

In this sacrament we enjoy the hospitality of God, who gives himself to us in Jesus Christ, crucified and risen. Thus breaking bread and distributing it—the act of attending lovingly to those in need—is an intrinsic dimension of the Eucharist. (J3 129)

In his certainty that his prayer would be heard, the Lord gave his body and blood to the disciples during the Last Supper in anticipation of the Resurrection: both Cross and Resurrection are intrinsic to the Eucharist—without them there would be no Eucharist. (J3 142)

Christian prayer for the Lord's return always includes the experience of his presence. It is never purely focused on the future. The words of the risen Lord make the point: "I am with you always, to the close of the age" (Mt 28:20). He is with us *now*, and especially close in the eucharistic presence. (J3 289)

The happiness you are seeking, the happiness you have a right to enjoy has a name and a face: it is Jesus of Nazareth, hidden in the Eucharist. Only he gives the fullness of life to humanity! With Mary, say your own "yes" to God, for he wishes to give himself to you. (G 39)

By making the bread into his Body and the wine into his Blood, he anticipates his death, he accepts it in his heart, and he transforms it into an action of love. What on the outside is simply brutal violence — the Crucifixion — from within becomes an act of total self-giving love. This is the substantial transformation which was accomplished at the Last Supper. (G 57)

We call this action "Eucharist," which is a translation of the Hebrew word *beracha* — thanksgiving, praise, blessing, and a transformation worked by the Lord: the presence of his "hour." Jesus's hour is the hour in which love triumphs. In other words: it is God who has triumphed, because he is Love. (G 59)

The Eucharist must become the center of our lives. (G 60)

Do not be deterred from taking part in Sunday Mass, and help others to discover it too. This is because the Eucharist releases the joy that we need so much, and we must learn to grasp it ever more deeply, we must learn to love it. (G 60)

The Eucharistic celebration must continue in our lives: bring to all the joy of Christ that you have found here. (G 64)

At the school of the saints, let us fall in love with this sacrament! Let us participate in Holy Mass with recollection, to obtain its spiritual fruits, let us nourish ourselves with this Body and Blood of Our Lord, to be ceaselessly fed by divine grace! (H 83)

Adore the Eucharist so as to increase in faith, to advance in the practice of the virtues, and to make reparation for offenses to the Most Holy Sacrament. (H 149)

It is comforting to know that many groups of young people have rediscovered the beauty of praying in adoration before the Most Blessed Sacrament.... I pray that this Eucharistic "springtime" may spread increasingly in every parish. (H 152)

Fidelity to the encounter with Christ in the Eucharist in Holy Mass on Sunday is essential for the journey of faith, but let us also seek to pay frequent visits to the Lord present in the Tabernacle! (H 153)

The Eucharist is an extraordinary gift of love that God continually renews to nourish our journey of faith, to strengthen our hope, and to inflame our charity, to make us more and more like him. (H 157)

Adoration means entering the depths of our hearts in communion with the Lord, who makes himself bodily present in the Eucharist. In the monstrance, he always entrusts himself to us and asks us to be united with his Presence, with his risen Body. (I 22)

What is the essential? The essential means never leaving a Sunday without an encounter with the Risen Christ in the Eucharist; this is not an additional burden but is light for the whole week. (H 241)

The Eucharistic table ... anticipates in a most eloquent way what the Lord promised in his "Sermon on the Mount": possession of the Kingdom of Heaven, participation in the meal of the heavenly Jerusalem. Let us pray that this be done for all. (HM 11-3-12)

Where is there a people to whom God is as close as our God is to us? In the Eucharist this has become the full reality. (HM 9-2-12)

It is in the Eucharist that the transformation of the gifts of this earth takes place — the bread and wine — whose aim is to transform our life and thereby to inaugurate the transformation of the world. (HM 6-23-11)

The words "to receive communion," referring to the act of eating the Bread of the Eucharist, are beautiful and very eloquent. In fact, when we do this act we enter into communion with the very life of Jesus, into the dynamism of this life which is given to us and for us. From God, through Jesus, to us: a unique communion is transmitted through the Blessed Eucharist. (HM 6-23-11)

Whereas food for the body is assimilated by our organism and contributes to nourishing it, in the case of the Eucharist it is a different Bread: it is not we who assimilate it but it assimilates us in itself, so that we become conformed to Jesus Christ, a member of his Body, one with him. (HM 6-23-11)

From the Sacrament of the Altar we have learned and are constantly learning that sharing, love, is the path to true justice. (HM 6-23-11)

Jesus desires us, he awaits us. But what about ourselves? Do we really desire him? Are we anxious to meet him? Do we desire to encounter him, to become one with him, to receive the gifts he offers us in the Holy Eucharist? Or are we indifferent, distracted, busy about other things? (HM 4-21-11)

The Eucharist is the mystery of the profound closeness and communion of each individual with the Lord and, at the same time, of visible union between all. The Eucharist is the sacrament of unity. It reaches the very mystery of the Trinity and thus creates visible unity. (HM 4-21-11)

"This is a hard saying; who can listen to it" (Jn 6:60). The reaction of the disciples—many of whom abandoned Jesus—to his discourse of the Bread of Life in the Synagogue of Capernaum is not very different from our own resistance to the total gift he makes of himself. For truly accepting this gift means losing oneself, letting oneself be involved and transformed. (HM 9-11-11)

Where should we start from, from what source, in order to recover and to reaffirm the primacy of God? From the Eucharist; here God makes himself so close that he makes himself a friendly presence that transforms. (HM 9-11-11)

Eucharistic communion, dear friends, wrenches us from our individualism, communicates to us the spirit of Christ dead and risen, and conforms us to him. It closely unites us with our brethren in that mystery of communion, which is the Church, where the one Bread makes many one body (1 Cor 10:17). (HM 9-11-11)

A Eucharistic spirituality is the soul of an ecclesial community which surmounts divisions and antagonism and appreciates the diversity of charisms and ministries, putting them at the service of the Church, of her vitality and mission. (HM 9-11-11)

There is nothing authentically human that does not find in the Eucharist the form it needs to be lived to the full: may daily life therefore become a place of spiritual worship, in order to live in all circumstances the primacy of God, as part of a relationship with Christ and as an offering to the Father. (HM 9-11-11)

The Man-God we shall see nailed to the Cross. The same Redeemer is present in the Sacrament of the Eucharist. (G 23)

The fact is that the Fathers of the Church were practically unanimous in understanding the fourth petition of the Our Father as a eucharistic petition; in this sense the Our Father figures in the Mass liturgy as a eucharistic table-prayer. (J2 154)

The miraculously multiplied bread harks back to the miracle of manna in the desert and at the same time points beyond itself: to the fact that man's real food is the Logos, the eternal Word, the eternal meaning, from which we come and toward which our life is directed. (J2 155 & 156)

The parable of the vine has a thoroughly eucharistic background. It refers to the fruit that Jesus brings forth: his love, which pours itself out for us on the Cross and which is the choice new wine destined for God's marriage feast with man. Thus we come to understand the full depth and grandeur of the Eucharist. (J2 261)

The Eucharist emphatically moves right to the center of Christian existence; here God does indeed give us the manna that humanity is waiting for, the true "bread of heaven"—the nourishment we can most deeply live upon as human beings. (J2 270)

Jesus, being the incarnate Word of God himself, is not just the Shepherd, but also the food, the true "pasture." He gives life by giving himself, for he *is* life (Jn 1:4, 3:36, 11:25). (J2 279)

Jesus interprets for us what happens at the institution of the Eucharist: He transforms the outward violence of the act

of crucifixion into an act of freely giving his life for others.
Jesus does not give *something*, but rather he gives himself.
And that is how he gives life. (J2 280)

Jesus interprets his own mystery, his own self, in light of
his gift of himself as the living bread. The people do not
like this; many go away. Jesus thereupon asks the Twelve:
Do you want to leave me as well? Peter answers: "Lord,
to whom shall we go? You have the words of eternal life"
(Jn 6:68). (J2 302)

The sacramental "mysticism," grounded in God's condescen-
sion towards us, operates at a radically different level and
lifts us to far greater heights than anything that any human
mystical elevation could ever accomplish. (D 8)

"Worship" itself, Eucharistic communion, includes the reality
of both being loved and of loving others in turn. A Eucharist
which does not pass over into the concrete practice of love
is intrinsically fragmented. (D 8)

The saints — consider the example of Blessed Teresa of
Calcutta — constantly renewed their capacity for love of
neighbor from their encounter with the Eucharistic Lord,
and conversely this encounter acquired its realism and
depth in their service to others. Love of God and love of
neighbor are thus inseparable, they form a single commandment. (D 10)

Communion with Christ creates among Christians a unity
of love. (C 138)

The Eucharist is also a visible process of gathering. In each
locality, as well as beyond all localities, it involves entering
into communion with the living God, who inwardly draws
people together. (J3 138)

A love for the Eucharist leads to a growing appreciation of the Sacrament of Reconciliation. Given the connection between these sacraments, an authentic catechesis on the meaning of the Eucharist must include a call to pursue the path of penance (1 Cor 11:27-29). (AE 2-22-07)

The Church comes into being from the Eucharist. She received her unity and her mission from the Eucharist. She is derived from the Last Supper, that is to say, from Christ's death and Resurrection, which he anticipated in the gift of his Body and Blood. (J3 138)

SELECTED
SPIRITUAL
TOPICS

PRAYER

Watch and pray that you may not enter
into temptation. — Mark 14:38

Indeed, without sufficient recollection it is impossible to approach the supreme mystery of God and of his revelation....Without prayer there is no experience of God. (J 70 & C 22)

The mystery of prayer, of the personal knowledge of Jesus, is concealed in charity: simple prayer that strives only to move the divine Teacher's heart. So it is that one's own heart opens, one learns from him his own kindness, his love. (C 72)

The believer—and all of us, as Christians and Muslims, are believers—...knows that, despite his weakness, he can count on the spiritual power of prayer. (G 75)

From conversion to mystic union with Christ Crucified to the inexpressible. A very lofty journey, whose secret is constant prayer. (H 127)

The more we love God and enter into intimacy with him in prayer, the more he makes himself known to us, setting our hearts on fire with his love. (H 177)

Dedicate the right time to prayer, to this openness to God, to this journey, in order to seek God, to see him, to discover his friendship, and so to find true life. (H 191)

Time devoted to prayer is not time wasted, it is time in which the path of life unfolds, the path unfolds to learning from God an ardent love for him, for his Church, and practical charity for our brothers and sisters. (H 192)

158   SELECTED SPIRITUAL TOPICS

No soul anxious for perfection fails to practice prayer daily,
mental prayer, an ordinary means that enables the disciple of
Jesus to live in intimacy with the divine Teacher. (H 197 & 198)

Cultivate a life of prayer, for it is through prayer that we
speak to God and that God speaks to us. (H 222)

Prayer . . . enables one to open oneself to divine grace in
order to do God's will every day and to obtain one's own
sanctification. (H 229)

By withdrawing into silence and solitude, human beings, so
to speak, "expose" themselves to reality in their nakedness, to
that apparent "void" . . . in order to experience instead the Fullness, the presence of God, of the most real Reality that exists
and that lies beyond the tangible dimension. (HM 10-23-11)

If being human is essentially about relation to God, it is
clear that speaking with, and listening to, God is an essential part of it. This is why the Sermon on the Mount also
includes a teaching about prayer. The Lord tells us how we
are to pray. (J2 128)

The more God is present in us, the more we will really be
able to be present to him when we utter the words of our
prayers. But the converse is also true: Praying actualizes
and deepens our communion of being with God. (J2 130)

Prayer, as a means of drawing ever-new strength from Christ,
is concretely and urgently needed. People who pray are
not wasting their time, even though the situation appears
desperate and seems to call for action alone. (D 20)

The Christian who prays does not claim to be able to change
God's plans or correct what he has foreseen. Rather, he
seeks an encounter with the Father of Jesus Christ, asking
God to be present with the consolation of the Spirit to him
and his work. (D 21)

When no one listens to me anymore, God still listens to me. When I can no longer talk to anyone or call upon anyone, I can always talk to God. When there is no longer anyone to help me deal with a need or expectation that goes beyond the human capacity for hope, he can help me. (s 16)

It is only the prayerful soul that can progress in spiritual life. (H 32)

Prayer nourished by Sacred Scripture and particularly by assiduous recourse to the Psalms always has a central place as the essential sustenance for all. (c 16)

This is important for us today, too, even though we are not monks: to know how to make silence within us to listen to God's voice, to seek, as it were, a "parlor" in which God speaks with us: learning the Word of God in prayer and in meditation is the path to life. (c 137)

You can once again have a moving experience of prayer as dialogue with God, the God who we know loves us and whom we in turn wish to love. (G 36)

Prayer (is) a loving relationship that impels man to speak gently with the Lord, creating an ineffable joy that sweetly enfolds the soul. (H 32)

Prayer requires an atmosphere of silence, which does not mean distance from external noise but, rather, is an interior experience that aims to remove the distractions caused by a soul's anxieties, thereby creating silence in the soul itself. (H 32)

Prayer is life and develops gradually, in pace with the growth of Christian life: it begins with vocal prayer, passes through interiorization by means of meditation and recollection, until it attains the union of love with Christ and with the Holy Trinity. (H 190)

In the development of prayer, climbing to the highest steps does not mean abandoning the previous type of prayer. Rather, it is a gradual deepening of the relationship with God that envelops the whole of life. (H 190)

Among the thousands of activities and multiple distractions that surround us, we must find moments for recollection before the Lord every day, in order to listen to him and speak with him. (H 198)

We must always reserve the time necessary to be in communion of prayer with our Lord. (H 221 & 222)

Praying without ceasing means: never losing contact with God, letting ourselves be constantly touched by him in the depths of our hearts and, in this way, being penetrated by his light. (HM 1-6-12)

It is important for everyone, in fact, to learn ever better how to "remain" with the Lord daily in personal encounters, to allow his love to take hold of them and to be proclaimers of the Gospel. (HM 11-4-11)

Again and again the Gospels note that Jesus withdrew "to the mountain" to spend nights in prayer "alone" with his Father . . . they give us a glimpse into Jesus's filial existence, into the source from which his action and teaching and suffering sprang. This "praying" of Jesus is the Son conversing with the Father. (J2 7)

In the Our Father . . . Jesus intends to teach disciples of all times how to pray; he intends to place them before the face of God, thus guiding them along the path to life. (J2 70)

This is what prayer really is — being in silent inward communion with God. It requires nourishment, and that is why we need articulated prayer in words, images, or thoughts. (J2 130)

Our praying can and should arise above all from our heart, from our needs, our hopes, our joys, our sufferings, from our shame over sin, and from our gratitude for the good. It can and should be a wholly personal prayer. (J2 130)

We also constantly need to make use of those prayers that express in words the encounter with God experienced both by the Church as a whole and by individual members of the Church. For without these aids to prayer, our own praying and our image of God become subjective and end up reflecting ourselves more than the living God. (J2 130)

In the formulaic prayers that arose first from the faith of Israel and then from the faith of praying members of the Church, we get to know God and ourselves as well. They are a "school of prayer" that transforms and opens up our life. (J2 130)

Normally, thought precedes word: it seeks and formulates the word. But praying the Psalms and liturgical prayer in general is exactly the other way round: The word, the voice, goes ahead of us, and our mind must adapt to it. (J2 131)

God has come to our aid: He himself provides the words of our prayer and teaches us to pray. Through the prayers that come from him, he enables us to set out toward him; by praying together with the brothers and sisters he has given us, we gradually come to know him and draw closer to him. (J2 131)

The Psalms are words that the Holy Spirit has given to men; they are God's Spirit become word. We thus pray "in the Spirit," with the Holy Spirit. This applies even more, of course, to the Our Father. When we pray the Our Father, we are praying to God with words given by God. (J2 131)

When we pray the Our Father, Jesus's promise regarding the true worshipers, those who adore the Father "in spirit and in truth" (Jn 4:23), is fulfilled in us. Christ, who is the truth, has given us these words, and in them he gives us the Holy Spirit. (J2 131)

The words of the Our Father are signposts to interior prayer, they provide a basic direction for our being, and they aim to configure us to the image of the Son. The meaning of the Our Father goes much further than the mere provision of a prayer text. It aims to form our being, to train us in the inner attitude of Jesus (Phil 2:5). (J2 132)

In prayer we must learn what we can truly ask of God— what is worthy of God. We must learn that we cannot pray against others. We must learn that we cannot ask for the superficial and comfortable things that we desire at this moment—that meagre, misplaced hope that leads us away from God. We must learn to purify our desires and our hopes. (s 17)

For prayer to develop this power of purification, it must on the one hand be something very personal, an encounter between my intimate self and God, the living God. On the other hand it must be constantly guided and enlightened by the great prayers of the Church and of the saints, by liturgical prayer, in which the Lord teaches us again and again how to pray properly. (s 17)

Praying must always involve this intermingling of public and personal prayer. This is how we can speak to God and how God speaks to us. In this way we undergo those purifications by which we become open to God and are prepared for the service of our fellow human beings. (s 17)

The Holy Spirit, that is, the Spirit of the Father and of the Son, is henceforth as it were the soul of our soul, the most secret part of our being, from which an impulse of prayer rises ceaselessly to God, whose words we cannot even begin to explain. (J 121)

The ascent to the peak of contemplation . . . can be achieved by those who abandon themselves to God. (C 19)

In the first place prayer is an act of listening, which then must be expressed in action. The Lord is waiting every day for us to respond to his holy admonitions by our deeds. (C 22)

Man seeks God better and finds him more easily in prayer than in discussion. In the end, the truest figure of a theologian and of every evangelizer remains the Apostle John, who laid his head on the Teacher's breast. (C 161)

Prayer, the self-opening of the human spirit to God, is true worship. The more man becomes "word"—or rather: the more his whole existence is directed toward God—the more he accomplishes true worship. (J3 233 & 234)

I am convinced that if more and more people unite themselves interiorly to the Lord's prayer "that all may be one" (Jn 17:21), then this prayer, made in the Name of Jesus, will not go unheard. (G 87)

Prayer is the soul of every activity: a prayer that listens to the word of God, that is satisfied in contemplating his grandeur, that does not withdraw into self but is pleased to abandon itself to God. (H 209)

Do we really have room for God when he seeks to enter under our roof? Do we have time and space for him? Do we not actually turn away God himself? We begin to do so when we have no time for God. (HM 12-24-12)

One does not evangelize by oneself . . . proclamation must always be preceded, accompanied and followed by prayer. (HM 10-23-11)

Every monastery—male or female—is an oasis in which the deep well, from which to draw "living water" to quench our deepest thirst, is constantly being dug with prayer and meditation. (HM 10-23-11)

We are at our most attentive when we are driven by inmost need to ask God for something or are prompted by a joyful heart to thank him for good things that have happened to us. (J2 129)

The more the depths of our souls are directed toward God, the better we will be able to pray. The more prayer is the foundation that upholds our entire existence, the more we will become men of peace. (J2 129 & 130)

Jesus's entire ministry arises from his prayer, and is sustained by it. Essential events in the course of his journey, in which his mystery is gradually unveiled, appear in this light as prayer events. (J2 132)

Personal prayer, nourished by the Lord's word, frequent reception of the sacraments, and the spiritual guidance of enlightened people are the means to discover and follow God's voice. (H 58)

Listening to God becomes living with God, and leads from faith to love. (J2 32)

THE CATHOLIC CHURCH

*So now I say to you: You are Peter and on this rock I
will build my Church. And the gates of the underworld
can never hold out against it.* —Matthew 16:18

The Twelve Apostles are the most evident sign of Jesus's
will regarding the existence and mission of his Church, the
guarantee that between Christ and the Church there is no
opposition: despite the sins of the people who make up the
Church, they are inseparable. (J 10)

A slogan that was popular some years back: "Jesus, yes.
Church, no," is totally irreconcilable with the intention of
Christ. This individualistically chosen Jesus is an imaginary
Jesus. We cannot have Jesus without the reality he created
and in which he communicates himself. (J 10)

Between the Son of God-made-flesh and his Church there
is a profound, unbreakable, and mysterious continuity by
which Christ is present today in his people. He is always
contemporary with us; he is always contemporary with the
Church, built on the foundation of the Apostles and alive
in the succession of the Apostles. (J 11)

The Church, a community gathered by the Son of God who
came in the flesh, will live on through the passing times,
building up and nourishing the communion in Christ and
in the Holy Spirit to which all are called and in which they
can experience the salvation given by the Father. (J 16)

The Apostles and their successors are the custodians and
authoritative witnesses of the deposit of truth consigned to
the Church and are likewise the ministers of charity. These
are two aspects that go together. (J 22)

This permanent actualization of the active presence of the Lord Jesus in his People, brought about by the Holy Spirit and expressed in the Church through the apostolic ministry and fraternal communion, is what, in a theological sense, is meant by the term "Tradition." (J 26 & 27)

Tradition ... is not merely the material transmission of what was given at the beginning to the Apostles, but the effective presence of the Crucified and Risen Lord Jesus, who accompanies and guides in the Spirit the community he has gathered together. (J 27)

Tradition is the practical continuity of the Church, the Holy Temple of God the Father, built on the foundation of the Apostles and held together by the cornerstone, Christ, through the life-giving action of the Spirit. (J 27)

The Lord founded the Church, as we have seen, by calling together the Twelve, who were to represent the future People of God. Faithful to the Lord's mandate, after his Ascension, the Twelve first made up their number by appointing Matthias in Judas's place (Acts 1:15-26). (J 34)

The successors of the Apostles were later called Bishops, *episcopoi*. The role of *episcope* was entrusted to them ... succession in the role of Bishop is presented as the continuity of the apostolic ministry, a guarantee of the permanence of the apostolic Tradition, word, and life, entrusted to us by the Lord. (J 35 & 36)

While there is no lack of unworthy and traitorous Christians in the Church, it is up to each of us to counterbalance the evil done by them with our clear witness to Jesus Christ, our Lord and Savior. (J 108)

History shows us that one usually reaches Jesus by passing through the Church! In a certain sense, this proved true ... also for Paul, who encountered the Church before he encountered Jesus. (J 124)

From this derive the greatness and nobility of the Church, that is, of all of us who are part of her: from our being members of Christ, an extension as it were of his personal presence in the world. And from this, of course, stems our duty truly to live in conformity with Christ. (J 126)

A relationship of communion is at stake: the so-to-speak *vertical* communion between Jesus Christ and all of us, but also the *horizontal* communion between all who are distinguished in the world by the fact that they "call on the name of Our Lord Jesus Christ" (1 Cor 1:2). (J 127)

The Lord ... leads his Church, generation after generation, availing himself equally of men and woman who are able to make their faith and Baptism fruitful for the good of the entire Ecclesial Body and for the greater glory of God. (J 154)

To this day, images still speak to the hearts of believers; they are not relics of the past. Cathedrals are not medieval monuments but rather houses of life in which we feel "at home" and where we meet God and one another. (C 36)

Christ the Bridegroom wants a hard-working Church ... intent on integrating the Gospel into their social fabric and cultural institutions. (C 77)

This great Bishop [Boniface] did not omit to encourage the foundation of various male and female monasteries so that they would become like beacons, so as to radiate human and Christian culture and the faith. (C 81)

The Church is in Christ's hands ... the Church can never be separated from Jesus Christ. (C 90)

There is a certain visibility of God in the world, in the Church, that we must learn to perceive. (C 97)

Precisely with regard to the Church, we men and women are prompted to see above all the sins and negative side, but with the help of faith, which enables us to see in an authentic way, today and always we can rediscover the divine beauty in her. (C 98)

The most important value in a theological controversy (is) to preserve the Church's faith and to make the truth in charity triumph. Today, too, may this be the attitude with which we confront one another in the Church, having as our goal the constant quest for truth. (C 173)

The strength of the Romanesque style and the splendor of the Gothic cathedrals remind us that . . . the way of beauty is a privileged and fascinating path on which to approach the mystery of God. (C 183)

The sacraments are presented with a language interwoven with symbols and images capable of speaking directly to the human heart. . . . The sacraments (are) a cause of grace; they are truly able to communicate divine life. (C 188 & 214)

It is important to recognize how precious and indispensable for every Christian is the sacramental life in which the Lord transmits this matter in the community of the Church and touches and transforms us. (C 214)

The world's own efforts lead to disunion, as we can all see. Inasmuch as the world is operative in the Church, in Christianity, it leads to schisms. Unity can only come from the Father through the Son. (J3 95)

Through the humanly inexplicable unity of Jesus's disciples down the centuries, Jesus himself is vindicated. It can be seen that he is truly the "Son." Hence God can be recognized as the creator of a unity that overcomes the world's inherent tendency toward fragmentation. (J3 96)

With the Eucharist, the Church herself was established. Through Christ's body, the Church became one, she became herself, and at the same time, through his death, she was opened up to the breadth of the world and its history. (J3 138)

In this double outpouring of blood and water, the Fathers saw an image of the two fundamental sacraments — Eucharist and Baptism — which spring forth from the Lord's pierced side, from his heart. This is the new outpouring that creates the Church and renews mankind. (J3 226)

Jesus identifies himself with the persecuted Church. (J3 264)

In the Church and through the Church you will meet Christ, who is waiting for you. (G 36)

There is much that could be criticized in the Church. We know this and the Lord himself told us so: it is a net with good fish and bad fish, a field with wheat and darnel. (G 54)

It is actually consoling to realize that there is darnel in the Church. In this way, despite all our defects, we can still hope to be counted among the disciples of Jesus, who came to call sinners. (G 55)

The Church is like a human family, but at the same time she is also the great family of God, through which he establishes an overarching communion and unity that embraces every continent, culture and nation. (G 55)

The Lord sees and loves each individual person, and we are all the living Church for one another. (G 56)

The Catholic Church is committed—I reaffirm this again today—to tolerance, respect, friendship and peace between all peoples, cultures and religions. (G 71)

We want to be a Church open to the future, rich in promises for the new generations. It is not a matter of pandering to youth, which is basically ridiculous, but of a true youthfulness that flows from the well-springs of eternity, that is ever new, that derives from the transparency of Christ in his Church: this is how he gives us the light to continue. (G 96)

In the Church there are many ways ... all together they converge in a symphony of faith. The local Churches and movements are not in opposition to one another, but constitute the living structure of the Church. (G 99)

Everything must have its own order.... The law of the Church is necessary to give shape to renewal. (H 17)

Only in Heaven will we understand how much the prayer of cloistered religious effectively accompanies apostolic action! To each and every one of them I address my grateful and affectionate thoughts. (H 28)

The Church is made more luminous and beautiful by the fidelity to their vocation of those sons and daughters of hers who not only put the evangelical precepts into practice but, by the grace of God, are called to observe their counsels and thereby, with their poor, chaste, and obedient way of life, to witness to the Gospel as a source of joy and perfection. (H 39)

The grace of the Holy Spirit (is) given to all who believe in Christ. The written and oral teaching of the doctrinal and moral truths transmitted by the Church is united to this grace. (H 76)

Down through history innumerable women have been

fascinated by love for Christ, who, with the beauty of his Divine Person, fills their hearts. And the entire Church, through the mystical nuptial vocation of consecrated virgins, appears as what she will be forever: the pure and beautiful Bride of Christ. (H 103)

I recall with admiration and gratitude the women's and men's cloistered monasteries. Today more than ever they are oases of peace and hope, a precious treasure for the whole Church, especially since they recall the primacy of God and the importance, for the journey of faith, of constant and intense prayer. (H 162)

I see with joy so many children who are following God's word at various levels, preparing for First Communion, for Confirmation and, after Confirmation, for life. Welcome! I am happy to see a living Church! (HM 12-16-12)

The universality of the Church flows from the universality of God's unique plan of salvation for the world. This universal character emerges clearly on the day of Pentecost, when the Spirit fills the first Christian community with his presence, so that the Gospel may spread to all nations. (HM 11-24-12)

The Church's universal mission does not arise from below, but descends from above, from the Holy Spirit: from the beginning it seeks to express itself in every culture so as to form the one People of God.... It is like yeast oriented towards a universal horizon. (HM 11-24-12)

Around the Apostles, Christian communities spring up, but these are "the" Church which is always the same, one and universal, whether in Jerusalem, Antioch, or Rome. And when the Apostles speak of the Church, they are not referring to a community of their own, but to the Church of Christ. (HM 11-24-12)

The Church is one, holy, catholic, and apostolic, she reflects in herself the source of her life and her journey: the unity and communion of the Trinity. (HM 11-24-12)

The new evangelization applies to the whole of the Church's life. (HM 10-28-12)

The Council documents are a luminous expression of the Gospel and the faith of the Church, as is the Catechism of the Catholic Church. (HM 10-11-12)

This has continued to be the Church's mandate: she does not preach what the powerful wish to hear. Her criterion is truth and justice even if it is unpopular and against human power. (HM 7-15-12)

The Lord calls everyone, distributing different gifts for different tasks in the Church. He calls people to the priesthood and to the consecrated life and he calls them to marriage and to commitment as lay people, both in the Church herself and in society. It is important that the wealth of gifts be fully accepted. (HM 7-15-12)

The Council documents contain an enormous wealth for the formation of the new Christian generations, for the formation of our consciences. Consequently, read (them). (HM 7-15-12)

Read the *Catechism of the Catholic Church* and thereby rediscover the beauty of being Christian, of being Church, of living the great "we" that Jesus formed around him in order to evangelize the world. (HM 7-15-12)

The Church also participates in the mystery of divine motherhood, through preaching, which sows the seed of the Gospel throughout the world, and through the sacraments, which communicate grace and divine life to men. (HM 1-1-12)

The Holy Spirit gives life to the Church. She is not born from the human will, from man's reflection, from his ability or from his organizational capacity, if this were so she would have ceased to exist long ago, as happens with all that is human. Instead the Church is the body of Christ, enlivened by the Holy Spirit. (HM 6-12-11)

The Church was catholic from the very outset . . . her universality is not the result of the successive inclusion of various communities. Indeed, from the first moment the Holy Spirit created her as the Church of all peoples; she embraces the whole world, surmounts all distinctions of race, class and nation. (HM 6-12-11)

Since the beginning the Church has been one, catholic and apostolic: this is her true nature and must be recognized as such. She is not holy because of her members' ability but because God himself, with his Spirit, never ceases to create her, purify her and sanctify her. (HM 6-12-11)

"They gathered together in prayer with Mary in the Upper Room, waiting for the promised event" (Acts 1:14). Remaining together was the condition given by Jesus for them to experience the coming of the Paraclete, and prolonged prayer served to maintain them in harmony with one another. We find here a formidable lesson for every Christian community. (HM 6-5-11)

Man is the way of the Church, and Christ is the way of man. (HM 5-1-11)

The Church is not some kind of association that concerns itself with man's religious needs but is limited to that objective. No, she brings man into contact with God and thus with the source of all things. (HM 4-23-11)

Life in the Church's faith involves more than a set of feelings and sentiments and perhaps moral obligations. It embraces man in his entirety, from his origins to his eternal destiny. (HM 4-23-11)

We have special reasons to praise God for his mystery of salvation, active in the world through the ministry of the Church. We have so many reasons to thank the Lord for what our ecclesial community, at the heart of the universal Church, is accomplishing in the service of the Gospel. (HM 12-31-11)

I encourage parish communities and other ecclesial groupings to engage in continuing reflection on ways to promote a better understanding and reception of the sacraments, by which man comes to share in the very life of God. (HM 12-31-11)

Every Gospel missionary must always bear in mind this truth: it is the Lord who touches hearts with his word and with his Spirit, calling people to faith and to communion in the Church. (HM 10-23-11)

The mission of the Church, like that of Christ, is essentially to speak of God, to remember his sovereignty, to remind all, especially Christians who have lost their own identity, of the right of God to what belongs to him, that is, our life. (HM 10-23-11)

No vocation in the People of God is on the fringes. We are one body, in which every member is important and has the same dignity, and is inseparable from the whole. (HM 10-23-11)

The Church is the "universal sacrament of salvation" (*Lumen Gentium,* 48), existing for sinners, for us, in order to open up to us the path of conversion, healing and life. That is the Church's great perennial mission, entrusted to her by Christ. (HM 9-22-11)

Many people see only the outward form of the Church.... If to this is added the sad experience that the Church contains both good and bad fish, wheat and darnel, and if only these negative aspects are taken into account, then the great and beautiful mystery of the Church is no longer seen. (HM 9-22-11)

To abide in Christ means to abide in the Church as well. The whole communion of the faithful has been firmly incorporated into the vine, into Christ. In Christ we belong together. Within this communion he supports us, and at the same time all the members support one another. (HM 9-22-11)

The Church is not simply a human institution, like any other. Rather, she is closely joined to God. Christ himself speaks of her as "his" Church. Christ cannot be separated from the Church any more than the head can be separated from the body (1 Cor 12:12). The Church does not draw her life from herself, but from the Lord. (HM 8-21-11)

As the Successor of Peter, let me urge you to strengthen this faith which has been handed down to us from the time of the Apostles. Make Christ, the Son of God, the center of your life. But let me remind you that following Jesus in faith means walking at his side in the communion of the Church. (HM 8-21-11)

I ask you, dear friends, to love the Church which brought you to birth in the faith, which helped you to grow in the knowledge of Christ and which led you to discover the beauty of his love. Growing in friendship with Christ necessarily means recognizing the importance of joyful participation in the life of your parishes. (HM 8-21-11)

The holiness of the Church is above all the objective holiness of the very person of Christ, of his Gospel and his sacraments, the holiness of that power from on high which enlivens and impels it. (HM 8-21-11)

When we say the word *our,* we say Yes to the living Church in which the Lord wanted to gather his new family. In this sense, the Our Father is at once a fully personal and a thoroughly ecclesial prayer. (J2 141)

God, though so remote from us, has made himself our neighbor in Jesus Christ. He pours oil and wine into our wounds, a gesture seen as an image of the healing gift of the sacraments, and he brings us to the inn, the Church, in which he arranges our care and also pays a deposit for the cost of that care. (J2 200 & 201)

One of the soldiers "pierced his side with a spear, and at once there came out blood and water" (Jn 19:34). There is no doubt that John means to refer here to the two main sacraments of the Church — Baptism and the Eucharist — which spring forth from Jesus's opened heart and thus give birth to the Church from his side. (J2 242 & 243)

Union with Christ is also union with all those to whom he gives himself. I cannot possess Christ just for myself; I can belong to him only in union with all those who have become, or who will become, his own. Communion draws me out of myself towards him, and thus also towards unity with all Christians. We become "one body." (D 8)

Love of neighbor, grounded in the love of God, is first and foremost a responsibility for each individual member of the faithful, but it is also a responsibility for the entire ecclesial community at every level: from the local community to the particular Church and to the Church universal in its entirety. (D 11)

Within the community of believers there can never be room for a poverty that denies anyone what is needed for a dignified life.... The Church cannot neglect the service of charity any more than she can neglect the Sacraments and the Word. (D 12)

A just society must be the achievement of politics, not of the Church. Yet the promotion of justice through efforts to bring about openness of mind and will to the demands of the common good is something which concerns the Church deeply. (D 15)

The Church is one of those living forces: she is alive with the love enkindled by the Spirit of Christ. This love does not simply offer people material help, but refreshment and care for their souls, something which often is even more necessary than material support. (D 16)

Whoever loves Christ loves the Church, and desires the Church to be increasingly the image and instrument of the love which flows from Christ. The personnel of every Catholic charitable organization want to work with the Church and therefore with the Bishop. (D 19)

The Church does not have technical solutions to offer and does not claim "to interfere in any way in the politics of States." She does, however, have a mission of truth to accomplish, in every time and circumstance, for a society that is attuned to man, to his dignity, to his vocation. Without truth, it is easy to fall into an empiricist and skeptical view of life. (CV 4)

If development were concerned with merely technical aspects of human life, and not with the meaning of man's pilgrimage through history in company with his fellow human beings, nor with identifying the goal of that journey, then the Church would not be entitled to speak on it. (CV 7)

The Church's social doctrine, which has "an important inter-disciplinary dimension," can exercise, in this perspective, a function of extraordinary effectiveness. It allows faith, theology, metaphysics and science to come together in a col-laborative effort in the service of humanity. It is here above all that the Church's social doctrine displays its dimension of wisdom. (CV 15 & 16)

The Church's social doctrine came into being in order to claim "citizenship status" for the Christian religion. Denying the right to profess one's religion in public and the right to bring the truth of faith to bear upon public life has negative consequences for true development. (CV 31)

The Church has formulated an Apostolic Succession, the episcopal ministry, in the awareness that the Word and the witness go together; that is, the Word is alive and present only thanks to the witness, so to speak, and receives from the witness its interpretation. But the witness is only such if he witnesses to the Word. (G 84)

Every charism is destined to build up the Church. (H 138)

Saint Augustine could say: "as much as any man loves the Church, so much has he the Holy Spirit." (HM 9-22-11)

THE MASS

A man once had a great supper. —Luke 14:16

An integral part of liturgical celebration is the Word of God. (C 115)

To celebrate the liturgy in the awareness of God's presence, with that dignity and beauty which make a little of his splendor visible, is the commitment of every Christian trained in his faith. (C 98)

The liturgy, lived in its true spirit, is always the fundamental school for living the Christian faith, a "theological" faith which involves you in your whole being—spirit, soul and body—to make you living stones in the edifice of the Church. (HM 12-1-12)

God is found above all in praising him, not only in reflection; and the liturgy is not something made by us, something invented in order to have a religious experience for a certain period of time; it is singing with the choir of creatures and entering into cosmic reality itself. (C 28)

Intensify (y)our friendship with the Lord, especially through daily prayer and attentive, faithful, and active participation in Holy Mass. The liturgy is a great school of spirituality. (H 113)

In periods of work, with its frenetic pace, and in holiday periods we must reserve moments for God. We must open our lives to him, addressing to him a thought, a reflection, a brief prayer, and above all we must not forget Sunday as the Lord's Day, the day of the liturgy. (C 116)

Christian life does not develop unless it is nourished by participation in the liturgy—particularly at Sunday Mass—and by personal daily prayer, by personal contact with God. (H 198)

It is in the Church that God is present, offers himself to us
in the Holy Eucharist, and remains present for adoration.
In the Church God speaks to us; in the Church God "walks
beside us".... In the Church we receive God's forgiveness
and learn to forgive. (CV 98)

Let us discover the intimate riches of the Church's liturgy
and its true greatness: it is not we who are celebrating for
ourselves, but it is the living God himself who is preparing
a banquet for us. (G 60)

We are often so oppressed, understandably oppressed, by
the immense social needs of the world and by all the organizational and structural problems that exist that we set
aside worship as something for later.... Nothing is more
important than worship. (G 95)

I had discovered the beauty of the Liturgy, and I came to love
it more and more because I felt that divine beauty appears
in it and that Heaven unfolds before us. (I 23)

May Holy Mass be the center of your Sunday. It should be
rediscovered and lived as a day for God and of community,
a day in which to praise and celebrate the One who died
and rose for our salvation and asks us to live together in
the joy of a community open and ready to accept every
person. (HM 12-16-12)

The community is built with the contribution that each one
makes, with the commitment of all; and I am thinking in a
special way of the field of catechesis, that of the liturgy and
that of charity: pillars that support Christian life. (HM 12-11-11)

Do not lose your sense of Sunday and be faithful to the
Eucharistic gathering. The early Christians were prepared

to give their lives for this. They realized that this is life and gives life. (HM 12-11-11)

The fight for Sunday is another of the Church's major concerns in the present day, when there is so much to upset the rhythm of time that sustains community. (J2 121)

Let us ask the Lord to grant that we may overcome our limits, our world, to help us to encounter him, especially at the moment when he places himself into our hands and into our heart in the Holy Eucharist. (HM 12-24-12)

I would like to remind you all of the importance and the centrality of the Eucharist in personal and community life. (HM 12-16-12)

The Eucharistic table . . . anticipates in a most eloquent way what the Lord promised in his "Sermon on the Mount": possession of the Kingdom of Heaven, participation in the meal of the heavenly Jerusalem. Let us pray that this be done for all. (HM 11-3-12)

Stay firm in the faith, rooted in Christ through the Word and the Eucharist; be people who pray, in order to remain linked forever to Christ, like branches to the vine. (HM 7-15-12)

The love of Christ is not reserved for a few but is destined for all. . . . It is in the Eucharist that the transformation of the gifts of this earth takes place — the bread and wine — whose aim is to transform our life and thereby to inaugurate the transformation of the world. (HM 6-23-11)

The fact that the Sacrament of the Altar acquired the name "Eucharist" — "thanksgiving" — expresses precisely this: that changing the substance of the bread and wine into the Body and Blood of Christ is the fruit of the gift that Christ made of himself, the gift of Love stronger than death. (HM 6-23-11)

The words "to receive communion," referring to the act of eating the Bread of the Eucharist, are beautiful and very eloquent. In fact, when we do this act we enter into communion with the very life of Jesus. (HM 6-23-11)

The Eucharist, while it unites us to Christ, also opens us to others, makes us members of one another: we are no longer divided but one in him. Eucharistic communion not only unites me to the person I have beside me and with whom I may not even be on good terms, but also to our distant brethren in every part of the world. (HM 6-23-11)

It is necessary for each and every one of us to let ourselves be taught by Jesus, as the two disciples of Emmaus were: first of all by listening to and loving the word of God.... Then it is necessary to sit at table with the Lord, to share the banquet with him, so that his humble presence in the Sacrament of his Body and Blood may restore to us the gaze of faith. (HM 5-8-11)

The Sabbath is the day of rest. But something quite unprecedented happened in the nascent Church: the place of the Sabbath, the seventh day, was taken by the first day. As the day of the liturgical assembly, it is the day for encounter with God through Jesus Christ who as the Risen Lord encountered his followers on the first day, Sunday, after they had found the tomb empty. (HM 4-23-11)

The encounter (with the Risen Lord) happens afresh at every celebration of the Eucharist, when the Lord enters anew into the midst of his disciples and gives himself to them, allows himself, so to speak, to be touched by them, sits down at table with them. (HM 4-23-11)

Jesus desires us, he awaits us. But what about ourselves? Do we really desire him? Are we anxious to meet him? Do we desire to encounter him, to become one with him, to receive the gifts he offers us in the Holy Eucharist? Or are we indifferent, distracted, busy about other things? (HM 4-21-11)

From Jesus's banquet parables we realize that he knows all about empty places at table, invitations refused, lack of interest in him and his closeness. For us, the empty places at the table of the Lord's wedding feast, whether excusable or not, are no longer a parable but a reality. (HM 4-21-11)

Those who do not live their faith as love are not ready for the banquet.... Eucharistic communion requires faith, but faith requires love, otherwise, even as faith, it is dead. (HM 4-21-11)

The ultimate purpose of Eucharistic transformation is our own transformation in communion with Christ. The Eucharist is directed to the new man, the new world, which can only come about from God, through the ministry of God's Servant. (HM 4-21-11)

With the Eucharist, the Church is born. All of us eat the one bread and receive the one body of the Lord; this means that he opens each of us up to something above and beyond us. He makes all of us one. (HM 4-21-11)

The Eucharist is a mystery of the profound closeness and communion of each individual with the Lord and, at the same time, of visible union between all. The Eucharist is the sacrament of unity. It reaches the very mystery of the Trinity and thus creates visible unity. (HM 4-21-11)

After Peter was converted, he was called to strengthen his brethren. It is not irrelevant that this task was entrusted to him in the Upper Room. The ministry of unity has its visible place in the celebration of the Holy Eucharist. (HM 4-21-11)

We can understand what it means to live as branches of Christ, the true vine, and to bear fruit.... Such is the Church, this communion of life with Jesus Christ and for one another, a communion that is rooted in baptism and is deepened and given more and more vitality in the Eucharist. "I am the true vine" actually means: "I am you and you are I"—an unprecedented identification of the Lord with us, with his Church. (HM 9-22-11)

In Jesus the ultimate and definitive word of God becomes flesh, comes to meet us as a Person. He, the eternal Word, is the true manna, the Bread of Life (Jn 6:32-35) and doing the works of God is believing in him (Jn 6:28-29). (HM 9-11-11)

At the Last Supper Jesus summed up the whole of his life in an act that is inscribed in the great paschal blessing to God, an act that he lives as Son in thanksgiving to the Father for his immense love. (HM 9-11-11)

Eucharistic communion wrenches us from our individualism, communicates to us the spirit of Christ dead and risen, and conforms us to him. It closely unites us with our brethren in that mystery of communion, which is the Church, where the one Bread makes us one body (1 Cor 10:17). (HM 9-11-11)

Being nourished by Christ is the way not to be foreign or indifferent to the fate of the brethren, but rather to enter into the same logic of love and of the gift of the sacrifice of the Cross; anyone who can kneel before the Eucharist, who receives the Body of the Lord, cannot but be attentive in the ordinary daily routine to situations unworthy of the human being. (HM 9-11-11)

A Eucharistic spirituality is the true antidote to the individualism and selfishness that often mark daily life. It leads to the rediscovery of giving freely, to the centrality of relationships, starting with the family, and pays special attention to alleviating the wounds of broken families. (HM 9-11-11)

There is nothing authentically human that does not find in the Eucharist the form it needs to be lived to the full: may daily life therefore become a place of spiritual worship, in order to live in all circumstances the primacy of God. (HM 9-11-11)

Jesus continues, in the sacrament of the Eucharist, to love us "to the end," even to offering us his body and his blood. What amazement must the Apostles have felt in witnessing what the Lord did and said during that Supper! What wonder must the eucharistic mystery also awaken in our own hearts! (AE 2-22-07)

In the sacrament of the altar, the Lord meets us, men and women created in God's image and likeness (Gen 1:27), and becomes our companion along the way. In this sacrament, the Lord truly becomes food for us, to satisfy our hunger for truth and freedom. (AE 2-22-07)

From the varied forms of the early centuries... from the clear indications of the Council of Trent and the Missal of Saint Pius V to the liturgical renewal called for by the Second Vatican Council: in every age of the Church's history the Eucharistic celebration, as the source and summit of her life and mission, shines forth in the liturgical rite in all its richness and variety. (AE 2-22-07)

Deepen (your) understanding of the relationship between the Eucharistic mystery, the liturgical action, and the new spiritual worship which derives from the Eucharist as the sacrament of charity. (AE 2-22-07)

The Church's faith is essentially a Eucharistic faith, and it is especially nourished at the table of the Eucharist. Faith and the sacraments are two complementary aspects of ecclesial life. (AE 2-22-07)

The Sacrament of the Altar is always at the heart of the Church's life. Thanks to the Eucharist, the Church is reborn ever anew! The more lively the Eucharistic faith of the People of God, the deeper is its sharing in ecclesial life in steadfast commitment to the mission entrusted by Christ to his disciples. (AE 2-22-07)

When, on the banks of the Jordan, John the Baptist saw Jesus coming towards him, he cried out: "Behold, the Lamb of God, who takes away the sin of the world" (Jn 1:29). It is significant that these same words are repeated at every celebration of Holy Mass, when the priest invites us to approach the altar. (AE 2-22-07)

By (Christ's) command to "do this in remembrance of me" (Lk 22:19; 1 Cor 11:25), he asks us to respond to his gift and to make it sacramentally present. In these words the Lord expresses, as it were, his expectation that the Church, born of his sacrifice, will receive this gift, developing under the guidance of the Holy Spirit the liturgical form of the sacrament. (AE 2-22-07)

The substantial conversion of bread and wine introduces within creation the principle of a radical change, a sort of "nuclear fission," to use an image familiar to us today, which penetrates to the heart of all being . . . a process leading ultimately to the transfiguration of the entire world, to the point where God will be all in all (1 Cor 15:28). (AE 2-22-07)

The Church, (Christ's) Bride, is called to celebrate the Eucharistic banquet daily in his memory. She thus makes the redeeming sacrifice of her Bridegroom a part of human history and makes it sacramentally present in every culture. (AE 2-22-07)

The Eucharist is Christ who gives himself to us and continually builds us up as his body. Hence, in the striking interplay between the Eucharist which builds up the Church, and the Church herself which "makes" the Eucharist, the primary causality is expressed in the first formula: the Church is able to celebrate and adore the mystery of Christ present in the Eucharist precisely because Christ first gave himself to her in the sacrifice of the Cross. (AE 2-22-07)

It is significant that the Second Eucharistic Prayer, invoking the Paraclete, formulates its prayer for the unity of the Church as follows: "... may all of us who share in the body and blood of Christ be brought together in unity by the Holy Spirit".... The Eucharist is thus found at the root of the Church as a mystery of communion. (AE 2-22-07)

In the celebration of the Eucharist, the individual members of the faithful find themselves in their Church, that is, in the Church of Christ ... ecclesial communion is seen to be catholic by its very nature. (AE 2-22-07)

The loss of a consciousness of sin always entails a certain superficiality in the understanding of God's love. Bringing out the elements within the rite of Mass that express consciousness of personal sin and, at the same time, of God's mercy, can prove most helpful to the faithful. (AE 2-22-07)

Since the conditions for gaining an indulgence include going to confession and receiving sacramental communion, this practice can effectively sustain the faithful on their journey of conversion and in rediscovering the centrality of the Eucharist in the Christian life. (AE 2-22-07)

The divorced and remarried continue to belong to the Church, which accompanies them with special concern and encourages them to live as fully as possible the Christian life through regular participation at Mass, albeit without receiving communion. (AE 2-22-07)

If it is true that the sacraments are part of the Church's pilgrimage through history towards the full manifestation of the victory of the risen Christ, it is also true that, especially in the liturgy of the Eucharist, they give us a real foretaste of the eschatological fulfillment for which every human being and all creation are destined (Rom 8:19). (AE 2-22-07)

Perceive God's beauty itself in the beauty of our Churches, in our sacred music, and in the Word of God, letting him enter our being. Only in this way does our life become great, become true life. (C 116)

THE PAPACY

Feed my sheep. —John 21:17

Pray for the Successors of the Apostles, for all the Bishops and for the Successors of Peter, so that together they may truly be at the same time custodians of truth and love; so that, in this regard, they may truly be apostles of Christ and that his light, the light of truth and love, may never be extinguished in the Church or in the world. (J 23)

Jesus "looked at him and said, 'So you are Simon the son of John? You shall be called Cephas' (which means Peter)" (Jn 1:42). . . . It was not only a name; it was a "mandate" that *Petrus* received in that way from the Lord. (J 50)

Peter is responsible for guaranteeing communion with Christ with the love of Christ, guiding people to fulfill this love in everyday life. Let us pray that the Primacy of Peter, entrusted to poor human beings, will always be exercised in this original sense as the Lord desired and that its true meaning will therefore always be recognized by the brethren who are not yet in full communion with us. (J 53)

Exercising the Roman Primacy was as necessary then as it is today to serve communion, a characteristic of Christ's one Church, effectively. (C 10)

That so many young people have come to meet the Successor of Peter is a sign of the Church's vitality. I am happy to be with them, to confirm their faith and, God willing, to enliven their hope. (G 29)

The spontaneity of new communities is important, but it is also important to preserve communion with the Pope and with the Bishops. It is they who guarantee that we are not seeking private paths, but instead are living as God's great family, founded by the Lord through the twelve apostles. (G 61 & 62)

When controversies arise in the Church, the reference to the Petrine ministry guarantees fidelity to sound doctrine. (J3 263)

Thanks be to God the wise helmsmen of the Barque of Saint Peter, Pope Paul VI, and Pope John Paul II, on the one hand, defended the newness of the Council and, on the other, defended the oneness and continuity of the Church, which is always a Church of sinners and always a place of grace. (H 47)

It is only in the unity represented by Peter that we truly lead people to Christ. (HM 6-29-11)

"Blessed are you, Simon, son of Jonah! For flesh and blood has not revealed this to you, but my Father in heaven" (Mt 16:17). What did our heavenly Father reveal to Simon? That Jesus is the Christ, the Son of the living God. Because of this faith, Simon becomes Peter, the rock on which Jesus can build his Church. (HM 5-1-11)

Three times the Lord says to Peter: "Feed my lambs" (or sheep — Jn 21:15-17). Peter is very clearly being appointed as the shepherd of Jesus's sheep and established in Jesus's office as shepherd. (J2 276 & 277)

It is an expression of the prophetic task of the Supreme Pontiffs to give apostolic guidance to the Church of Christ and to discern the new demands of evangelization. (CV 6)

The Pope is with you! (HM 12-1-12)

Spiritual bonds ... unite the whole Church, brought to life by Christ and gathered around the Successor of Peter. (HM 12-1-12)

Between these two Popes, Paul VI and John Paul II, there was a deep and complete convergence, precisely upon Christ as the center of the cosmos and of history, and upon the apostolic eagerness to announce him to the world. (HM 10-11-12)

I have come among you as the Bishop of Rome and perpetuator of Peter's ministry, to strengthen you in faithfulness to the Gospel and in communion ... which must involve us all in a serious and well-coordinated service to the cause of the Kingdom of God. (HM 5-8-11)

Today the one proclaimed blessed (John Paul II) is a Pope, a Successor of Peter, one who was called to confirm his brethren in the faith. John Paul II is blessed because of his faith, a strong, generous and apostolic faith. (HM 5-1-11)

"I have prayed for you, that your faith may not fail; and when you have turned again, strengthen your brethren" (Lk 22:31). Today we are once more painfully aware that Satan has been permitted to sift the disciples before the whole world. And we know that Jesus prays for the faith of Peter and his successors. (HM 4-21-11)

Only by the prayer of the Lord and of the Church can the Pope fulfill his task of strengthening his brethren—of feeding the flock of Christ and of becoming the guarantor of that unity which becomes a visible witness to the mission which Jesus received from the Father. (HM 4-21-11)

Have courage! The Pope is close to you in his thoughts and prayers. Have courage! (HM 11-2-11)

The Church must be one around Peter. (HM 9-24-11)

Jesus responds to Peter's confession by speaking of the Church: "And I tell you, you are Peter, and on this rock I will build my Church." What do these words mean? Jesus builds his Church on the rock of the faith of Peter, who confesses that Christ is God. (HM 9-11-11)

SACRED SCRIPTURE

Heaven and earth will pass away; but my
words will not pass away. —Matthew 24:6

Scripture is not something of the past. The Lord does not speak in the past but speaks in the present, he speaks to us today, he enlightens us, he shows us the way through life, he gives us communion and thus he prepares us and opens us to peace. (J 19)

The key to understanding Sacred Scripture as the one Word of God is Christ, and with Christ, in his light, one understands the Old and New Testaments as "one" Sacred Scripture. The events of the Old and New Testaments go together; they are the way to Christ, although expressed in different signs and institutions. (C 74)

No one possesses the Gospel for himself alone but must perceive it as a gift for others too. (C 77)

The desire to know and to love God which comes to meet us through his words, which are to be received, meditated upon, and put into practice, leads us to seek to deepen our knowledge of the biblical texts in all their dimensions. (C 165)

Those who practice monastic theology insist (that) an intimate, prayerful disposition . . . must precede, accompany, and complete the study of Sacred Scripture. (C 165)

To those who know the meaning of history as described in the Bible, human events appear marked by divine Providence, in accordance with a clearly ordained plan. (C 187)

Jesus will ask his disciples: "Who do people say that I am? . . . Who do you say that I am?" (Mk 8:27). Who is Jesus?

Where is he from? The two questions are inseparably linked. The four Gospels set out to answer these questions. They were written in order to supply an answer. (J1 4)

The Psalms constantly offer new hope, however deep the surrounding darkness. In the early Church, Jesus was immediately hailed as the new David, the real David, and so the Psalms could be recited in a new way—yet without discontinuity—as prayer in communion with Jesus Christ. (J3 146)

The Psalms are deeply personal prayers, formed while wrestling with God, yet at the same time they are uttered in union with all who suffer unjustly, with the whole of Israel, indeed with the whole of struggling humanity, and so these Psalms always span past, present, and future. (J3 215)

Love for Sacred Scripture is so important . . . it is important to know the faith of the Church which opens up for us the meaning of Scripture. It is the Holy Spirit who guides the Church as her faith grows, causing her to enter ever more deeply into the truth (Jn 16:13). (G 61)

Both Jews and Christians recognize in Abraham their father in faith (Gal 3:7; Rom 4:11), and they look to the teachings of Moses and the Prophets. Jewish spirituality, like its Christian counterpart, draws nourishment from the psalms. (G 70 & 71)

The early Church primarily took a threefold decision: first, to establish the canon, thereby stressing the sovereignty of the Word and explaining that not only is the Old Testament "hai graphai," but together with the New Testament constitutes a single Scripture and is thus for us the master text. (G 84)

The Church remains the true, authentic home of the Gospel and of Scripture. (H 9)

The riches of Christ's word are inexhaustible. (H 46)

All that is truly rational is compatible with the faith revealed in the Sacred Scriptures. (H 62)

One must not read Sacred Scripture as one reads any kind of historical book . . . it is necessary to read it as the Word of God, that is, entering into a conversation with God. One must start praying and talking to the Lord: "Open the door to me." (I 67)

Meditate often on the events and words of the life of Jesus . . . be familiar with Sacred Scripture, always cherishing it in our hearts so that it may give direction to all our thoughts and all our actions. (H 168)

In pursuing ecumenical dialogue with such great hope, the reference to Sacred Scripture, interpreted in accordance with the Tradition of the Church, is an indispensable element of fundamental importance. (H 220)

Listening to and the reception of the word of God produces an inner transformation that leads us to holiness. (H 223)

The Church of Rome is called to proclaim and to witness tirelessly to the riches of Christ's Gospel. (HM 12-31-12)

The *evangelium*, the Gospel, is not just informative speech, but performative speech—not just the imparting of information, but action, efficacious power that enters into the world to save and transform. (J2 471)

Interpretation of Scripture can never be a purely academic affair, and it cannot be relegated to the purely historical. Scripture is full of potential for the future, a potential that can only be opened up when someone "lives through" and "suffers through" the sacred text. (J2 78)

First of all, it is important to listen as accurately as possible to Jesus's words as transmitted to us in Scripture. We must strive to recognize the thoughts Jesus wished to pass on to us in these words. (J2 133)

The universal character of the Gospel ... is meant for all the peoples of the earth. (J2 180)

We have good reason to be convinced that the Holy Scriptures are "inspired," that they matured in a special sense under the guidance of the Holy Spirit. (J2 182)

The parables constitute the heart of Jesus's preaching. While civilizations have come and gone, these stories continue to touch us anew with their freshness and their humanity. (J2 183)

We read the Bible, and especially the Gospels, as an overall unity expressing an intrinsically coherent message, notwithstanding their multiple historical layers. (J2 191)

If people do not believe the word of Scripture, then they will not believe someone coming from the next world either. The highest truths cannot be forced into the type of empirical evidence that only applies to material reality. (J2 216)

The Gospel itself opens up a path of understanding, which always remains bound to the scriptural word, and yet from generation to generation can lead, and is meant to lead, ever anew into the depth of all the truth. (J2 234)

Jesus attaches great importance to being in continuity with the Scripture, in continuity with God's history with men. (J2 246)

I urge you to become familiar with the Bible and to have it at hand so that it can be your compass pointing out the road to follow. By reading it, you will learn to know Christ. (I 67)

The whole Gospel of John, as well as the Synoptic Gospels and the entirety of the New Testament writings, justify faith in Jesus by showing that all the currents of Scripture come together in him, that he is the focal point in terms of which the overall coherence of Scripture comes to light — everything is waiting for him, everything is moving toward him. (J2 246)

The Lord always speaks in the present and with an eye to the future. He is also speaking with us and about us. If we open our eyes, isn't what He said in the parable actually a description of our present world? Isn't this precisely the logic of the modem age, of our age? (J2 257)

The real novelty of the New Testament lies not so much in new ideas as in the figure of Christ himself, who gives flesh and blood to those concepts — an unprecedented realism. (D 7)

It is also important to set aside a certain period each day for meditation on the Bible, so that the Word of God may be a light that illumines our daily pilgrimage on earth. (C 166)

Together with "apostolic succession," the early Church discovered (she did *not* invent) two further elements fundamental for her unity: the canon of Scripture and the so-called *regula fidei*, or "rule of faith." (J3 99)

The new reading of Scripture could begin only after the Resurrection, because it was only through the Resurrection that Jesus was accredited as the one sent by God. Now people had to search Scripture for both Cross and Resurrection, so as to understand them in a new way and thereby come to believe in Jesus as the Son of God. (J3 245)

You must not limit yourselves to hearing the Word, you must put it into practice ... let yourself be led by it! Let us pray to the Lord that this may happen, and that like this the truth may have power over us, and acquire power in the world through us. (HM 9-2-12)

What are "the springs of salvation"? They are the Word of God and the sacraments. Adults are the first who should nourish themselves at these sources.... If we cut ourselves off from this spring, we ourselves are the first to feel the negative effects and are no longer able to educate others. (HM 1-8-12)

Creation and Scripture, reason and faith, must come together, so as to lead us forward to the living God.... The great star, the true supernova that leads us on, is Christ himself. He is as it were the expression of God's love, which causes the great white light of his heart to shine upon the world. (HM 1-6-12)

In the Scriptures, in the Sacraments, in prayer, in the communion of saints, in the people who come to me, sent by him, I try to come to know the Lord himself more and more. (HM 6-29-11)

In the intimacy of the home do not be afraid to read the Sacred Scriptures, illuminating family life with the light of faith and praising God as Father. Be like a little Upper Room, like that of Mary and the disciples, in which to live unity, communion and prayer! (HM 6-5-11)

I break the bread of the Word and of the Eucharist with you, in the certainty—shared by us all—that without Christ, the Word and Bread of Life, we can do nothing (Jn 15:5). (HM 10-16-11)

The new evangelizers are called to walk first on this Way that is Christ, to make others know the beauty of the Gospel that gives life. (HM 10-16-11)

There is no loftier Gospel, there is no other Church to await. (H 45)

It is necessary to entrust oneself to Sacred Scripture alone, to the Word of the Lord, to look out on the horizon of faith with humility, in order to enter into the enormous immensity of the universal world, of the world of God. (C 71)

THE PRIESTHOOD

As the Father has sent me, even so I send you.
And when He had said this, he breathed on them, and
said to them: Receive the Holy Spirit. —John 20:21–22

If the family of God's children is to live in unity and peace, it needs someone to keep it in the truth and guide it with wise and authoritative discernment: this is what the ministry of the Apostles is required to do. (J 21 & 22)

Serve the Gospel with generosity, realizing that this also entails a service to the Church herself. (J 132)

The center of the Church is the Eucharist, where the Body of Christ and his Blood are made present through the priesthood, the Eucharist, and the communion of the Church. Wherever the priesthood and the Eucharist and the Church come together, it is there alone that the word of God also dwells. (H 17 & 18)

Let us ask God always to enrich the Church with authentic preachers of the Gospel. (H 28)

Pastoral ministry . . . must be more animated by the fire of the Holy Spirit, so as to inflame the hearts of the faithful who regularly take part in community worship and gather on the Lord's day to be nourished by his word and by the bread of eternal life. (HM 10-28-12)

"I no longer call you servants, but friends" (Jn 15:15). Sixty years on from the day of my priestly ordination, I hear once again deep within me these words of Jesus that were addressed to us new priests at the end of the ordination ceremony. (HM 6-29-11)

I know that forgiveness comes at a price: in his Passion he went down deep into the sordid darkness of our sins.... And by giving me authority to forgive sins, he lets me look down into the abyss of man, into the immensity of his suffering for us men, and this enables me to sense the immensity of his love. (HM 6-29-11)

(Our Lord) entrusts to me the words of consecration in the Eucharist. He trusts me to proclaim his word, to explain it aright and to bring it to the people of today. He entrusts himself to me. (HM 6-29-11)

"No longer servants, but friends": this saying contains within itself the entire program of a priestly life. What is friendship?—wanting the same things, rejecting the same things.... Friendship is a communion of thinking and willing. (HM 6-29-11)

(Christ) set out through the mountains and the deserts, in which his lamb, humanity, had strayed. It reminds us of him who took the lamb—humanity—me—upon his shoulders, in order to carry me home. It reminds us that we too, as shepherds in his service, are to carry others with us, taking them as it were upon our shoulders and bringing them to Christ. (HM 6-29-11)

I turn finally to you, dear brothers in the priestly ministry. Holy Thursday is in a special way our day. At the hour of the Last Supper, the Lord instituted the New Testament priesthood. "Sanctify them in the truth" (Jn 17:17), he prayed to the Father. (HM 4-21-11)

The apostolic community was united in prayer in the Upper Room with Mary, the mother of Jesus (Acts 1:12-14). This is a picture of the Church with deep roots in the paschal event: indeed, the Upper Room is the place where Jesus instituted the Eucharist and the priesthood during the Last Supper, and where, having risen from the dead, he poured out the Holy Spirit upon the Apostles. (HM 6-5-11)

With great gratitude for the vocation and with humility for all our shortcomings, we renew at this hour our "yes" to the Lord's call: yes, I want to be intimately united to the Lord Jesus, in self-denial, driven on by the love of Christ. (HM 4-21-11)

The Word of God ... invites us to meditate on the mission of pastors in the Christian community. From the dawn of the Church, importance was clearly given to the leaders of the first communities established by the Apostles for the proclamation of the Word of God through preaching and the celebration of the sacrifice of Christ, the Eucharist. (HM 11-4-11)

The apostolic vocation lives on thanks to the personal relationship with Christ, nourished by regular prayer and enlivened by the passion to spread the message received and the same experience of faith as the Apostles. (HM 11-4-11)

There are certain conditions to ensure growing harmony in priestly life with Christ ... aspiration to work with Jesus in spreading the Kingdom of God, pastoral duty freely given and the attitude of service. (HM 11-4-11)

First, in the call to the priestly ministry we meet Jesus and are drawn to him, struck by his words, his actions, and his person. It is to have the grace to distinguish his voice from so many other voices and to respond like Peter: "Lord, to whom shall we go? You have the words of eternal life" (Jn 6:68-69). (HM 11-4-11)

God the Father sent the Eternal Son into the world to bring about his plan of salvation. Jesus Christ established the Church so that it might extend in time the benefits of Redemption. The vocation of priests is rooted in the Father's action realized in Christ, through the Holy Spirit. (HM 11-4-11)

The Gospel minister is the one who lets himself be seized by Christ, who knows how to "stay" with him, who enters into harmony, into an intimate friendship with him, so that all is done "not by constraint but willingly" (1 Pet 5:2), according to his will of love, with great interior freedom and profound joy in the heart. (HM 11-4-11)

One should never forget that one comes into the priesthood through the Sacrament of Orders and this means exactly opening oneself to God's action by choosing daily to give oneself up for God and for one's brethren, according to the Gospel saying: "You received without pay, give without pay" (Mt 10:8). (HM 11-4-11)

The Lord's call to the ministry is not the fruit of special merit but a gift to be received and responded to by dedicating oneself not to one's own plan but to God's, in a generous and disinterested way. (HM 11-4-11)

We must never forget — as priests — that the only legitimate ascent to the ministry of the pastor is not that of success, but of the Cross. (HM 11-4-11)

Being a priest means being a servant also through an exemplary life. Be "examples to the flock" is the Apostle Peter's invitation (1 Pet 5:3). (HM 11-4-11)

Priests are stewards of the means of salvation, of the sacraments, especially the Eucharist and Reconciliation, not to dispense them according to their own will, but as humble servants for the good of the People of God. It is a life profoundly marked by this service. (HM 11-4-11)

Dear priests, I urge you to root your spiritual life ever more deeply in the Gospel, cultivating your inner life, an intense relationship with God and detaching yourselves with determination from a certain consumerist and worldly mentality, which is a recurrent temptation in the situation in which we live. (HM 10-9-11)

"The mystery of faith!" With these words, spoken immediately after the words of consecration, the priest proclaims the mystery being celebrated and expresses his wonder before the substantial change of bread and wine into the body and blood of the Lord Jesus, a reality which surpasses all human understanding. (AE 2-22-07)

Bishops have a pastoral duty of promoting within their Diocese a reinvigorated catechesis on the conversion born of the Eucharist, and of encouraging frequent confession among the faithful. All priests should dedicate themselves with generosity, commitment and competency to administering the sacrament of Reconciliation. (AE 2-22-07)

The intricate relationship between the Eucharist and the sacrament of Holy Orders clearly emerges from Jesus's own words in the Upper Room: "Do this in memory of me" (Lk 22:19). (AE 2-22-07)

On the night before he died, Jesus instituted the Eucharist and at the same time established the priesthood of the New Covenant. He is priest, victim and altar: the mediator between God the Father and his people (Heb 5:5-10), the victim of atonement (1 Jn 2:2, 4:10) who offers himself on the altar of the Cross. No one can say "this is my body" and "this is the cup of my blood" except in the name and in the person of Christ, the one high priest of the new and eternal Covenant (Heb 8:9). (AE 2-22-07)

The ordained minister also acts in the name of the whole Church, when presenting to God the prayer of the Church, and above all when offering the Eucharistic sacrifice. As a result, priests should be conscious of the fact that in their ministry they must never put themselves or their personal opinions in first place, but Jesus Christ. (AE 2-22-07)

The priest is above all a servant of others, and he must continually work at being a sign pointing to Christ, a docile instrument in the Lord's hands. This is seen particularly in his humility in leading the liturgical assembly. (AE 2-22-07)

The ministerial priesthood, through ordination, calls for complete configuration to Christ ... there is a need to reaffirm the profound meaning of priestly celibacy, which is rightly considered a priceless treasure. (AE 2-22-07)

Celibacy is really a special way of conforming oneself to Christ's own way of life. This choice has first and foremost a nuptial meaning; it is a profound identification with the heart of Christ the Bridegroom who gives his life for his Bride. (AE 2-22-07)

I reaffirm the beauty and the importance of a priestly life lived in celibacy as a song expressing total and exclusive devotion to Christ, to the Church and to the Kingdom of God.... Priestly celibacy lived with maturity, joy and dedication is an immense blessing for the Church and for society itself. (AE 2-22-07)

We need to have ever greater faith and hope in God's providence. Even if there is a shortage of priests in some areas, we must never lose confidence that Christ continues to inspire men to leave everything behind and to dedicate themselves totally to celebrating the sacred mysteries, preaching the Gospel and ministering to the flock. (AE 2-22-07)

I offer a special word of thanks to those ... priests who work faithfully and generously at building up the community by proclaiming the word of God and breaking the Bread of Life, devoting all their energy to serving the mission of the Church. (AE 2-22-07)

Let us thank God for all those priests who have suffered even to the sacrifice of their own lives in order to serve Christ. The eloquence of their example shows what it means to be a priest to the end. Theirs is a moving witness that can inspire many young people to follow Christ and to expend their lives for others, and thus to discover true life. (AE 2-22-07)

(God) grants me the almost frightening faculty to do what only he, the Son of God, can legitimately say and do: I forgive you your sins. He wants me—with his authority—to be able to speak, in his name, words that are not merely words, but an action, changing something at the deepest level of being. (HM 6-29-11)

I ask pastors to be vigilant with regard to the celebration of the sacrament of Reconciliation, and to limit the practice of general absolution exclusively to the cases permitted, since individual absolution is the only form intended for ordinary use. (AE 2-22-07)

I urge priests, especially ministers in charge of souls, to have an intense sacramental life in themselves in the first place in order to be of help to the faithful. (C 215)

THE SAINTS

The virtuous will shine like the sun in the kingdom of their Father. — Matthew 13:43

(The) important writers of the Eastern and Western Church in the Middle Ages (are so) because in their life and writings we see as in a mirror what it means to be Christian. (C 129)

By inviting us to venerate the mortal remains of the martyrs and saints, the Church does not forget that, in the end, these are indeed just human bones, but they are bones that belonged to individuals touched by the living power of God.... Christian Saints, having become partakers of the Resurrection of Christ, cannot be considered simply "dead"... relics or images are worthy of veneration. (G 40 & C 102)

The relics of the saints are traces of that invisible but real presence which sheds light upon the shadows of the world and reveals the Kingdom of Heaven in our midst. They cry out with us and for us: "Maranatha!" — "Come, Lord Jesus!" (G 40)

It is the great multitude of the saints — both known and unknown — in whose lives the Lord has opened up the Gospel before us and turned over the pages; he has done this throughout history and he still does so today. (G 53)

The saints and the blesseds did not doggedly seek their own happiness, but simply wanted to give themselves, because the light of Christ had shone upon them. (G 53)

(The saints) show us the way to attain happiness; they show us how to be truly human. Through all the ups and downs of history, they were the true reformers who constantly rescued it from plunging into the valley of darkness. (G 53)

The saints are the true reformers. Now I want to express this in an even more radical way: only from the saints, only from God does true revolution come, the definitive way to change the world. (G 53)

Let us look at the history of Christianity to see how history develops and how it can be renewed. It shows that saints, guided by God's light, are the authentic reformers of the life of the Church and of society. (H 7)

This comforting reality, namely, that in every generation saints are born and bring the creativity of renewal, constantly accompanies the Church's history in the midst of the sorrows and negative aspects she encounters on her path. (H 7)

The saints are the best interpreters of the Bible. As they incarnate the word of God in their own lives, they make it more captivating than ever, so that it really speaks to us. (H 20)

Love for the Lord and for neighbor, the search for God's glory and the salvation of souls in the lives of the saints always go hand in hand (H 23)

This is a characteristic of saints: they cultivate friendship because it is one of the noblest manifestations of the human heart and has something divine about it. (H 67)

How often in the history of the Church believers have met with hostility and even suffered persecution for their fidelity and devotion to Christ, to the Church, and to the Pope. We all look with admiration at these Christians, who teach us to treasure as a precious good faith in Christ and communion with the Successor of Peter, hence with the universal Church. (H 87)

Those who change the world for the better are holy; they transform it permanently, instilling in it the energies that only love inspired by the Gospel can elicit. The saints are mankind's great benefactors! (H 106)

God . . . gives us saints who speak to our hearts and offer us an example of Christian life to imitate. (H 107)

The saints never failed to find strength, consolation, and joy in the Eucharistic encounter. (H 153)

Even in the most difficult times, the Lord does not cease to bless his People, bringing forth Saints who give a jolt to minds and hearts, provoking conversion and renewal . . . and (who) still speak to us and impel us to walk courageously toward holiness, to be ever more fully disciples of the Lord. (H 154)

The whole of the Church's history is marked by these men and women who with their faith, with their charity, and with their life have been beacons for so many generations, as they are for us, too. (H 238)

The saints expressed in various ways the powerful and transforming presence of the Risen One. They let Jesus so totally overwhelm their life that they could say with Saint Paul, "it is no longer I who live, but Christ who lives in me" (Gal 2:20). (H 238)

During the Liturgical Year, the Church invites us to commemorate a host of saints, the ones, that is, who lived charity to the full, who knew how to love and follow Christ in their daily lives. They tell us that it is possible for everyone to take this road. (H 242)

In the Communion of Saints, canonized and not canonized, which the Church lives, thanks to Christ, in all her members, we enjoy their presence and their company and cultivate the firm hope that we shall be able to imitate their journey and share one day in the same blessed life, eternal life. (H 243)

The saints are God's true constellations, which light up the nights of this world, serving as our guides. Saint Paul, in his Letter to the Philippians, told his faithful that they must shine like stars in the world (Phil 2:15). Dear friends, this holds true for us, too. (HM 1-6-13)

The atmosphere of the Communion of Saints and the Commemoration of the Faithful Departed is present and alive in our hearts. (HM 11-3-12)

It has often been said that the real protagonists of the new evangelization are the saints: they speak a language intelligible to all through the example of their lives and their works of charity. (HM 10-28-12)

The saints are the true actors in evangelization in all its expressions. In a special way they are even pioneers and bringers of the new evangelization: with their intercession and the example of lives attentive to the inspiration of the Holy Spirit, they show the beauty of the Gospel. (HM 10-7-12)

The saints show us that it is possible and good to live in a relationship with God, to live this relationship in a radical way, to put it in first place, not just to squeeze it into some corner of our lives. (HM 9-24-11)

The saints help us to see that for his part God first reached out to us. We could not attain to him, we could not somehow reach out into the unknown, had he not first loved us.... He revealed and continues to reveal himself to us in Jesus Christ. (HM 9-24-11)

Still today Christ comes towards us, he speaks to every individual, just as he did in the Gospel, and invites every one of us to listen to him, to come to understand him and to follow him. This summons and this opportunity the saints acted on, they recognized the living God, they saw him, they listened to him and they went towards him, they traveled with him; they so to speak "caught" his contagious presence. (HM 9-24-11)

Even when they are few in number, saints change the world, and great saints remain as forces for change throughout history. (HM 9-24-11)

The figures of saints such as Francis of Assisi, Ignatius of Loyola, John of God, Camillus of Lellis, Vincent de Paul, Louise de Marillac...Teresa of Calcutta, to name but a few—stand out as lasting models of social charity for all people of good will. The saints are the true bearers of light within history, for they are men and women of faith, hope and love. (D 22)

The lives of the saints are not limited to their earthly biographies but also include their being and working in God after death. In the saints one thing becomes clear: those who draw near to God do not withdraw from men, but rather become truly close to them. (D 22 & 23)

The belief that love can reach into the afterlife, that reciprocal giving and receiving is possible, in which our affection for one another continues beyond the limits of death—this has been a fundamental conviction of Christianity throughout the ages and it remains a source of comfort today. (S 24)

Social doctrine is built on the foundation handed on by the Apostles to the Fathers of the Church, and then received and further explored by the great Christian doctors....It is attested by the saints and by those who gave their lives for Christ our Savior in the field of justice and peace. (CV 6)

In (the lives of the saints), as if in a great picture book, the riches of the Gospel are revealed. They are the shining path which God himself has traced throughout history and is still tracing today. (G 53)

The great men and women of prayer throughout the centuries were privileged to receive an interior union with the Lord that enabled them to descend into the depths beyond the word. They are therefore able to unlock for us the hidden treasures of prayer. (J2 133)

Holy images teach us to see God represented in the Face of Christ. After the Incarnation of the Son of God, it therefore became possible to see God in images of Christ and also in the faces of the Saints, in the faces of all people in whom God's holiness shines out. (C 97 & 98)

Let us invoke the Holy Spirit, the eternal youth of the Church: may he make each one aware of the urgent need to offer a consistent and courageous Gospel witness so that there may always be saints who make the Church resplendent . . . who can attract the world irresistibly to Christ and to his salvation. (H 13)

God's presence is always seen especially clearly in the saints. Their witness to the faith can also give us courage to begin afresh today. (HM 9-24-11)

The capacity to suffer for the sake of the truth is the measure of humanity. . . . The saints were able to make the great journey of human existence in the way that Christ had done before them, because they were brimming with great hope. (S 20)

Francis reminds us that the wisdom and benevolence of the Creator is expressed through creation. He understood nature as a language in which God speaks to us, in which reality becomes clear, and we can speak *of* God and *with* God. (H 21)

In the example of Blessed Teresa of Calcutta we have a clear illustration of the fact that time devoted to God in prayer not only does not detract from effective and loving service to our neighbor but is in fact the inexhaustible source of that service. (D 10)

The Church was built on the foundation of the Apostles as a community of faith, hope, and charity. Through the Apostles, we come to Jesus himself. (J 7)

What would the Church be without the new spirituality of the Cistercians, the Franciscans, and the Dominicans, the spirituality of Saint Teresa of Avila and Saint John of the Cross, and so forth? (H 46)

This Church does not stop at national borders, as we can see from the nationalities of the saints. (HM 9-24-11)

Let us too join our voices, minds and hearts in this hymn of thanksgiving for what divine grace worked in the Apostle to the Gentiles (Saint Paul) and for the wonderful saving plan which God the Father brings about in us through the Lord Jesus Christ. (HM 1-25-12)

God's radiance shines upon our world and shows us the path. The saints are stars of God, by whom we let ourselves be led to him for whom our whole being longs . . . may they continue to shine upon you and show you the path. (HM 1-6-12)

The profound sense of the Church's social presence derives from the Eucharist, as is testified by the great social saints who were always great Eucharistic souls. (HM 6-23-11)

From Elizabeth of Hungary, Vincent de Paul, Loiuse de Marillac, Camillus of Lellis to Mother Teresa—to recall but a few names—we see, lighting up the world, a radiant procession of helpers streaming forth from God's love for the suffering and the sick. For this we thank the Lord. (HM 4-21-11)

Dominic and Francis drew the power of their witness precisely from close communion with the Church and the Papacy. (H 9)